T0250439

Essential Project Management Skills

Essential Project Management Skills

Kerry R. Wills

CRC Press
Taylor & Francis Group
Boca Raton   London   New York

CRC Press is an imprint of the
Taylor & Francis Group, an **Informa** business

AN AUERBACH BOOK

CRC Press
Taylor & Francis Group
6000 Broken Sound Parkway NW, Suite 300
Boca Raton, FL 33487-2742

© 2010 by Taylor and Francis Group, LLC
CRC Press is an imprint of Taylor & Francis Group, an Informa business

Printed in the United States of America on acid-free paper
10 9 8 7 6 5 4 3 2 1

International Standard Book Number: 978-1-4398-2716-1 (Hardback)

Library of Congress Cataloging-in-Publication Data

Wills, Kerry R.
    Essential project management skills / Kerry R. Wills.
        p. cm.
    Includes bibliographical references and index.
    ISBN 978-1-4398-2716-1 (alk. paper)
    1. Project management. I. Title.

    HD69.P75W559 2010
    658.4'04--dc22   2009051623

Visit the Taylor & Francis Web site at
http://www.taylorandfrancis.com

and the CRC Press Web site at
http://www.crcpress.com

Contents

Preface

I have been in the project management field my entire career and have read many books and trade journals in this domain, the majority of which focused on specific techniques and disciplines, such as risk management or the creation of a work breakdown structure. I studied similar topics when I attended project management conferences and listened to the presenters. As a result, I started to develop my own presentations for project management conferences, which focused more on the skills required to be successful than on specific techniques to use.

While I was organizing my thoughts on my presentation topic and reflecting on my experiences, I realized that the landscape of projects was changing; therefore, the skills required to manage projects also needed to change. For example, based on my experience, it seemed that project managers who are more consultative in their style are more successful working in matrixed organizations and on complex programs. In the process of giving these presentations and interacting with the audience, it became equally apparent to me that there was a lot of content that could be discussed—so much, in fact, that this topic could fill a book. This gave rise to the present work.

The book is organized into four major sections. The first (Chapter 1) introduces the concepts related to the changing project landscape and their impact on projects. The second (Chapter 2) dives into the details of nine trends within the project landscape and describes the challenges created by these trends for project managers. Each trend is supplemented with a relevant case study. The third section (Chapter 3) outlines the skills required to be successful in this new environment and describes how to gain these skills, as well as techniques that can be applied. Each of these skills is also aligned with a case study in which the skills and techniques were used. The last section (Chapter 4) ties together the evolution of the project landscape, the challenges posed, and the new skills required. It also provides a checklist of the skills and techniques in the context of different project scenarios.

This is my first book, so I want to acknowledge the people who helped guide me through the creative process:

- My wife, Diane, for encouraging me to pursue my passion and for being supportive for the hours that I have dedicated toward writing the book
- My children, Stephanie and Matthew, for inspiring me every day
- My brother, Randy Wills, who helped me to think through the approach, content, and structure of the book over the last two years
- The contributors of the case studies (Vikas Bhor, Anneliese Dadras, Rob DeLaubel, Chris Richards, Kevin Savage, Carin Salonia, Partha Sastry, and Randy Wills), who helped supplement the key points with vivid examples taken from their experiences
- Konstantin Nikolaev, for taking my visual concepts and creating superb graphics from them that accent key points from the book
- John Wyzalek, for walking me through the process of creating and publishing my first book

Author

Kerry Wills has worked as a consultant and as a project manager for Fortune 500 companies on multi-million-dollar technology projects since 1995. During that time, he has gained experience in several capacities: program manager, project manager, architect, developer, business analyst, and tester. Having worked in each of these areas gives Kerry a deep understanding of all facets of an information technology project. He has planned and executed several large projects as well as remediated several troubled projects.

Kerry is a member of Mensa and has a unique perspective on project work, resulting in eight patents, published work in project management journals and books, and speaking engagements at more than twenty project management conferences and corporations around the world. He is a passionate speaker who has a reputation for delivering entertaining presentations combined with vivid examples from his experiences. He runs a project management blog called "Adventures in Project Management" at http://kerrywills.wordpress.com. He lives with his wife and two kids in Southington, Connecticut.

1

Background

The business landscape has been changing rapidly over the last several decades due to many factors, including global competition, more demanding shareholders, significant economic fluctuations, stock market volatility, and innovations in technology. This new environment has significantly accelerated the pace of change within businesses. To stay competitive, companies have had to transform their business agendas, which are heavily reliant on information technology (IT). They must focus on delivering more strategic and complex solutions with technology while at the same time reducing the cost to deliver IT services and increasing the productivity of IT resources. These transformation agendas have resulted in a different composition of technology projects, which poses a new set of challenges to the project management professionals who are accountable for the delivery of those projects.

An orchestra metaphor can be used to highlight the evolution of the project landscape. As Figure 1.1 highlights, in the "good old days" of IT projects, the project manager was like the conductor of an orchestra. The orchestra had dedicated musicians who played well together for many years under the sole direction of the conductor. They could write and play the music how they wanted, and the conductor just needed to wave his or her wand and the musicians responded in perfect harmony.

To continue with this metaphor, the landscape of the music business then began to change. Because of increased competition, the orchestra needed to evolve and deliver music in a cheaper and more efficient manner, so the management team of the orchestra started to introduce changes, as depicted in Figure 1.2:

1. The flute players were viewed as commodity resources that were being paid too much money, so that part of the orchestra was outsourced to a vendor who works in another country. They now

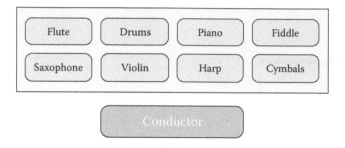

FIGURE 1.1
The good old days of IT project management.

videoconference with the orchestra, playing their flutes from a remote location that has cheaper wages.

2. The drummers were merged into a central drumming "pool" organization so that they could share the workload of other orchestras, as well as their drumming techniques with each other.

3. Because the drummers are now centralized, other conductors could instruct them on what to play and when. Because they are now receiving direction from several conductors, they have to prioritize their playing time to accommodate everyone's needs.

4. Management decided the piano players were not a strategic asset to the orchestra. So instead of having piano skills on the team, they purchased the "piano in a box" package from a vendor to play this portion of the music.

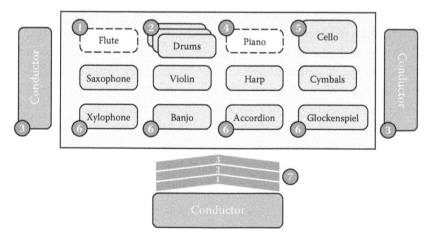

FIGURE 1.2
The new world of project management.

5. Management also decided to increase the scope of the fiddle player to take a more "enterprise" view of music. Therefore, they gave this musician responsibility for the cello, too.
6. The complexity of the music being played has increased, so new stakeholders have joined the team. These new team members include a banjo player, a xylophone player, an accordion player, and a glocken- spiel player.
7. Because of the tightening of the budget, management also intro- duced more process steps for the conductor to take before leading the orchestra. He or she can no longer conduct in the way that he or she sees fit; instead, the conductor now has to follow a standard method of conducting.

The orchestra metaphor is very relevant to how the project landscape has evolved over the last several years. The environment has changed from one where the project manager controlled all aspects of the project to one that looks similar to Figure 1.2, with many new stakeholders and chal- lenges that need to be managed. Some examples of the changes to projects are outlined in Table 1.1.

In order to be successful in the new project landscape, the skills of project management professionals and the techniques used must evolve. As Table 1.2 highlights, the project manager must move from a style of managing project plans and directing reports to a more influential and consultative approach that requires facilitation, negotiation, and relationship management.

This book focuses on the new world of projects and the skills and tech- niques required to be successful as a project manager. It is organized under two main topics:

- Chapter 2 will review the trends resulting from the business landscape, highlight the background and impacts they have on projects, and then identify the challenges they pose to IT project managers. Case studies will be used to highlight examples of these trends and impacts.
- Chapter 3 will describe the skill sets needed for project managers to succeed in the current environment, and provide techniques and approaches for success in today's world of the IT project manager. Case studies will be used to provide examples of the use of these skills and techniques and the associated outcomes.

This book is intended for any professional who is working in informa- tion technology and managing a component of work or a project. It is

TABLE 1.1

Examples of Changes in the Project Landscape

Project Landscape in the Past	Project Landscape in the Present
Resources reported to the project manager were dedicated to the project and located together	Less direct influence over resources: • Shared service/pooled organizations • Resources with several competing priorities • Off-shore developers • Co-sourcing models with vendors • Staff augmentation with consultants • Many more stakeholders to work with • "Borrowed" resources from other organizations • Part-time resources • Work-from-home resources • Mobile resources who may not be loyal to long-term commitments
Project team owned all assets and work and were focused on their priorities	Less direct control over the work being done, and additional rigor, process steps, and documentation are required: • Third-party vendors (buy vs. build) • Shared service organizations (e.g., infrastructure, support teams) • New procedures (e.g., Capability Maturity Model Integration [CMMI], Information Technology Infrastructure Library [ITIL], outsourcing agreements) with lead times • Focus on standards and solutions for the enterprise and not just the project • Regulations such as the Health Insurance Portability and Accountability Act (HIPAA) and Sarbanes–Oxley (SOX), with required documents
Project sponsor was owner and approved everything	Projects have more stakeholders to manage with different agendas: • Governance (architecture, financial, phase gates, etc.) • Many sponsors from different areas • Many competing priorities for the project sponsor's time and direction
Dedicated resources who worked at a company for a long time and had broad skills playing many roles on a team	Changing culture of the workforce: • Less loyalty to stay at one company (mobile workforce) • Resources and contractors who are experts in a specific skill or domain and not knowledgeable in a particular industry or company

TABLE 1.2

Changes in Skills Required for the New Project Landscape

Project Attribute	Project Landscape in the Past	Project Landscape in the Present
• Management of work	• Plan management—own and manage all activities with a dedicated staff	• Relationship management—many stakeholders and matrixed resources who are not fully dedicated to the project • Integration management—many involved organizations and subplans that require coordination • Political savvy and organizational navigation
• Interaction with resources	• Order giving—direct reports, so easy to influence • Tell resources to "just do it"	• Facilitation/negotiation—need to influence resources, who have competing priorities, without having formal reporting relationships
• Communications	• Report status to immediate management	• Stakeholder management • Proactive communication
• Sponsorship	• Receive direction from sponsor	• Facilitate several stakeholders

specifically targeted toward project managers who have a fundamental background in project management principles and want to augment their toolbox of skills and techniques around the delivery of projects in today's business environment. This book will not dive into project management techniques such as how to manage risks or set up a project plan, but rather will outline a framework and set of skills needed to successfully run a project given all of the recent trends and challenges.

2

Changing Project Landscape

2.1 OVERVIEW

The changing business environment has yielded four major trends that are impacting the landscape of IT delivery:

1. A focus on cost reduction of IT delivery
2. The increasing complexity of technologies used in IT delivery
3. The need for additional rigor on projects
4. A changing project workforce

Each of these trends will be reviewed in detail with explanations of their background and impact to the project landscape.

2.1.1 Trend 1—Reduce Cost

Technology is a significant part of companies' strategies and makes up a very large portion of companies' overall spend. According to a benchmark study done by Computer Economics, the companies surveyed spend anywhere from 1.5 to 2% of their total revenue on IT (Computer Economics, 2009). This can mean hundreds of millions or even billions of dollars being spent on technology for large companies.

As a result of the large expenditure, there is a lot of scrutiny from senior management and a subsequent pressure to keep costs down, or at the very least to grow these costs proportionally to revenue growth. This has led to two major approaches that companies are using around reducing the cost to deliver IT solutions:

1. Looking for cheaper resource options. IT organizations are outsourcing areas that they view as commodity roles, such as development and support work to offshore companies. In many cases these

resources are billed at rates that are 50% lower than those of local resources. These companies also propose higher-quality solutions due to increased rigor and consistency of delivery (as demonstrated by Capability Maturity ratings, as an example).

2. Pooling resources for economies of scale. For those skill sets not considered candidates for outsourcing, organizations have started to group similar expertise areas together. The premise is that by sitting together and pooling the work, more work can be produced for the same number of resources.

2.1.2 Trend 2—Increased Complexity

Another major trend is the increasing complexity of technology used by businesses. With the evolution of multilayered architectures and the Internet, the number of levels in the technology stack has grown significantly. There are also many different products in the marketplace, and companies usually have a "meatloaf" architecture, where several different products are integrated together to create solutions.

Also, companies have recognized technology as an enabler of strategy and competitive advantage. This has resulted in larger programs with broad impacts and many stakeholders to manage. It is not uncommon today for a company to have many multi-million-dollar and multiyear programs run concurrently.

Lastly, business processes and organizations are becoming more complex, and with that come more complex requirements for the technology to satisfy. Usually this means a lot of integration into other organizations and their systems, which may use different technologies.

To manage this complexity and the risk associated with it, companies have created several strategies:

1. Take an enterprise focus. In many large corporations, technology decisions were made in silos for long periods of time, which has resulted in having an inventory of redundant systems, competing technologies, and costly maintenance (more expensive licenses, the need for specialized resources, etc.). To get a better negotiating position with vendors and have less technologies to support, companies are moving to an enterprise view of their assets. This means selecting a standard for each type of technology and then putting governance in place to avoid creating similar problems in the future.

2. Hire vendor partners to help deliver (cosourcing). Because of the complexity of the environments, delivering large programs is difficult for companies who are not specialized in this area. They therefore work with a delivery partner in a cosourcing model to gain the delivery expertise, lower the risk of failure, and train their resources.
3. Utilize third-party vendor packages. Instead of building technology solutions locally, companies are moving to models where they are purchasing technology systems from third-party vendors.

2.1.3 Trend 3—Additional Rigor

Because of the increasing complexity, size, and number of stakeholders on IT projects, additional rigor is needed and asked for by management. There are two primary places where the rigor is focused:

1. Demand management and governance. Demand management is focused on controlling the amount of money spent on IT and ensuring the proper priority of work. IT is viewed as an investment and therefore needs to be managed as such. Governance is making sure that the projects make sense and that teams have completed work before moving on to the next phase.
2. Process and tools. To ensure consistency of delivery and predictability, there are many frameworks in existence for the delivery of IT solutions (CMMI, Information Technology Infrastructure Library (ITIL), etc.). All of these lay out a foundation for delivering and supporting IT solutions with standard deliverables and processes. There are also additional processes introduced by regulatory initiatives such as Sarbanes–Oxley.

2.1.4 Trend 4—Changing Workforce

On top of an increasingly complex technology environment and additional process steps the workforce that is used on IT projects is also changing. There are two significant trends in the project workforce:

1. Specialized resources. The increasing complexity of technology and business solutions has resulted in resources becoming specialized into a particular skill (such as business analysis) or technology (such as a database platform). The result has been fewer people who view the big picture of a project.

2. A more mobile workforce. The workforce used on projects today is much more mobile than was in the past. This is mainly due to the high demand for skilled resources, allowing people to jump to better opportunities, and reduced company loyalty, as a function of strategies such as outsourcing and vendor usage.

The remainder of Chapter 2 will break down the above-mentioned trends and describe the challenges posed to project management professionals. It will also highlight case studies to demonstrate examples of those challenges.

2.2 REDUCE COST: OUTSOURCING

In the pursuit of reducing project delivery costs, organizations are increasing their use of outsourcing for specific technology work. Outsourcing includes entering into a contract with a third-party company to transfer technology delivery services to an offshore location. Outsourcing companies offer many IT project roles, such as business analysts, developers, and testers, at a location where wages are lower than in the United States. In some cases the employees who get replaced are moved into other positions within their current company, and in some cases they are let go.

As Figure 2.1 shows, in a classic outsourcing model a majority of the development work gets subcontracted and moved to an offshore location. The team leader may stay as an employee, but in most cases there is also an onshore lead from the outsourcing company to coordinate the work with the offshore team.

There are several benefits that can be realized by outsourcing IT work:

- Reduce cost of IT delivery. Companies can pay anywhere from 30 to 70% less for development resources at an offshore location than they would for onshore resources. This is also known as salary arbitrage.
- Additional capacity for work. Outsourcing companies can be used as a variable staff pool that can ramp up and ramp down resources relatively quickly depending on the demand for work. This means that companies do not need to carry the cost to maintain employees when the demand for IT work is down.

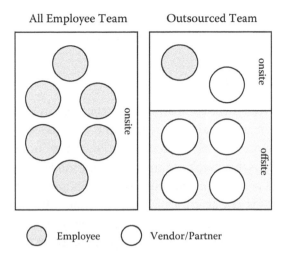

FIGURE 2.1
Standard outsourcing model.

- Access to a large talent base. Outsourcing companies have broad pools of resources in many IT domains that can be accessed and ramped up quickly.
- Transference of risk via contractual agreements. In some cases where a project is using new technologies or has a lot of risk, companies can set up the contract with the outsourcing vendor to accept some of this risk.
- Process rigor and high quality. Outsourcing companies use rigorous processes that are viewed as world class to ensure the quality of their deliverables.
- Knowledge in technical domains. In technologies where companies do not want to hire or build specialized skill sets, companies can utilize the outsourcing vendors to provide this expertise.
- Increased productivity. Because of the time zone difference for outsourcing companies, a project can be set up to work in several shifts to maximize the hours in a day working on the project.

Outsourcing of IT work has significantly increased over the last twenty years and is a reality in almost every major IT project today. Therefore, project managers need to understand the mechanics of outsourcing and the challenges that it poses.

While the main value proposition seems straightforward—pay less for resources—the reality of implementation is not as transparent or easy to quantify. There is a resulting increase in the amount of rigor and planning that a project needs to do and that a project manager needs to manage.

2.2.1 Additional Attention

The offshore development companies are structured in a way to take very detailed documentation and then develop the code based on those specifications. This requires a level of documentation that prior projects have not needed. On projects that didn't use an outsourcing model, developers were sitting with the rest of the team and could ask questions in real time, so detailed documentation was not as critical. With the time difference and physical location difference the interaction model has changed, and therefore more diligence is needed around documented specifics. There is also the process of knowledge transfer, which is making an investment in time to transfer the necessary company, project, and system knowledge to the offshore resources.

There are other logistical actions required as well, such as procurement and contractual processes to set up the financial arrangements and logistics with the outsourcing vendors. Offshore developers also usually require special access rights for company systems that need to be designed, set up, approved, and implemented. For example, a company may not want an offshore resource to have access to specific client/customer account information, such as social security number.

All of these new rigors require additional planning up front, which the project manager needs to account for in his or her project plan and schedule. They also require additional company resources for contract management, procurement, knowledge transfer, detailed documentation, quality reviews, billing, and vendor account management. These are stakeholders that the project manager needs to negotiate with, work with to set up the arrangement, and plan into his or her project plan and resource plan. The cost savings from using an offshore partner is somewhat offset with the additional work and planning that the project manager now needs to manage and contemplate.

2.2.2 Intangibles

There are also many intangible implications of outsourcing project delivery work. Most outsourcing companies are in different locations across the world. This can result in team members working in a different time zone, which poses a logistical and communication challenge since direct access to team members is limited. For example, during the testing phase of a project the onshore team may find a defect, but then need to wait until the next day when the offshore team can receive it, fix it, and then post it back (assuming there are no questions or follow-up activities).

There may also be cultural differences between the onshore and offshore teams. For example, in some cultures it is acceptable to be late to meetings, whereas this may be viewed as unprofessional at certain companies. Other cultures may also be reluctant to raise issues quickly because it is seen as not being able to manage their work, which means that by the time the issues are recognized, they are usually critical.

Because outsourcing has increased so rapidly over the last two decades there is a rush to find adequately skilled resources in the outsourcing country. This usually results in labor being pulled from one company to another, and therefore turnover is high. This poses a significant risk to a project manager who has resources dedicated to his or her project that were already brought up to speed on the project and the company.

If outsourcing is not used as additional capacity, but to replace current employees, there may also be morale issues with the local team. Usually the people responsible for transferring knowledge are those people who are affected, so they are not very motivated to do a thorough job in explaining the nuances of the business. Additionally, documentation may be limited, so the outsourcing company may have a hard time gaining a deep level of expertise. With lost experience the team may not be able to leverage the knowledge of past mistakes, which would doom the team to repeat them. Companies also have a distinct culture, which is something intangible that a specification document will not capture. All of this may result in decreased quality of work and mismanaged expectations.

In addition, with remote/offshore workers there is a loss in face-to-face time with the project team and forming personal relationships that can be gained and fostered more easily in person. There is an intangible benefit of working with a person and having face-to-face time where interpersonal bonds are formed. Communications can be a problem, and oftentimes the intent of a particular requirement or discussion can be lost by not being physically in the same location or being able to see body movement or facial expressions during difficult conversations. By having a very detailed specification as the primary means of communication in an offshore model, the business user's intent might be lost because the dialogue might not take place where perhaps an easier (and cheaper) solution is proposed by the developer working on the specific project.

The project manager must be sensitive to these intangible items and keep a constant pulse on the team to gauge when there may be challenges.

This then requires the project manager to not just focus on status, but to proactively be engaged in these risk areas to ensure that intagible risks are being managed. It also means that the project manager must focus on the people as much as on the process of being on the look out for morale issues and sensitivity to cultural differences.

Case Study: Setting Up and Then Working in a Sourcing Environment

Contributed by Anneliese Dadras

I had been at my position as a program manager for a few years when I was presented with "the golden opportunity." My company was entertaining a sourcing arrangement as an option to have more flexibility and greater diversity of the workforce. I was asked to participate in the evaluation, including negotiations, and help keep everything on track.

I was excited—it seems that sourcing is the hot new trend. This was a pretty major arrangement, and allowed me the opportunity to learn about sourcing from working with it. I was to partner with a seasoned executive that had almost single-handedly sourced a whole division in his last position. My job was to follow this individual around, keep the teams focused, and help where possible.

Little did I know how large this sourcing initiative would be; I seemed to be witnessing a large-scale effort that although organized, was highly chaotic. There was not much that I could share with other employees at my company, as many of the meetings and conversation were confidential. This did create stress and a little strain from my colleagues, and I found it odd that I could not disclose my day to even my closest confidant.

I thought that my past experiences had prepared me for this work. Before my current role, I had spent many years as a project manager. I had led both large and small initiatives—good and bad. The part I had not anticipated was the high degree of confidentiality, and how separated I felt from those who could be potentially impacted by my work.

When negotiations started, I was finally shoulder to shoulder with executives who had deep experience in sourcing organizations. I had a bird's-eye view at the table, and in a way I was honored and excited to learn about this new way to work. I had the opportunity to observe and to grow, and although there were many long nights and endless hours in meetings, I also felt that I was witnessing something unique to my career. The contract that was being formed bonded two separate companies together, and defined how hundreds of people would be working for the next seven years.

On the other hand, this was an uncomfortable situation for me personally—I was working with colleagues who would potentially be impacted by the very meetings that I was scheduling, coordinating, and privy to. My work was not always fun, and I looked for solace that a "greater good" might eventually come about for everyone involved.

In the end, the newspapers hailed the contract that was made as the largest of its kind. All the hard work had borne fruit—both companies were satisfied, and impacted employees received a very generous offer that was flexible and fair. Many former colleagues chose to work with the new sourcing partner, and some were glad that they had the opportunity to work for a significant player in the sourcing industry.

I now had experience with the negotiations and understood the mechanics of the deal. This allowed me to land a new role on the governance team. My job would be to govern the relationship, and to raise and track compliance issues that arose between the two companies. Now, I would be monitoring my former friends and workmates. It was a new role for me, but everyone was experiencing change. We all looked to the future and started to migrate to the new way of work.

Great change does not occur without discomfort. The largest change was that former employees now worked for the sourcing company. Although we were still on one big team, over time we began to realize that we truly were working for two different companies. New management soon arrived from the sourcing partner, and a new layer of oversight appeared. My former colleagues now had different managers and new objectives. Although we all knew from the start that it would never be the same, there was turmoil in that we didn't know where we were going. We were all in the same journey together, but didn't know our destination.

My role had new challenges. Employees that used to be my work colleagues were now the same persons that I governed. I now needed to define and create reports to track their progress, and to develop a process for alerting my management when we fell short. My world was changing, and although it was exciting and new, it also left me confused and unsure. One thing that I was certain about: I was not alone.

One of my first new challenges was to lead a project between our companies that defined the policies and procedures that we would together follow going forward. I was excited to work with my new project manager, until I learned that she worked 500+ miles from my home office. None of my 20+ years of project management would prepare me for this situation. How could someone lead a team remotely and never meet her teammates? I remember meeting her for my first phone interview, and wondering how I got myself into this situation. My many years of project management experience relied on face-to-face contact, evaluating body language, and the ability to "show up" at someone's desk to talk if a project was running late or an issue needed to be escalated. I realized that if I was going to be successful in my new environment, I was going to need to change in ways I hadn't thought necessary before.

Project management was more complicated than it was before. There were more project managers engaged than we ever had before. This is because for one project, we often needed a project manager to oversee our company's work, but the sourcing partner also needed its own project manager to oversee its work. This can be confusing, and leads to some very big meetings when discussing status. However, given that the sourcing partner has a commitment to deliver on its service level agreement, and that on-time delivery of projects is a measurement that it owes to us, it is understandable. We are one big team, but we are also two companies with independent goals, objectives, and ways of working. In the new world, it was very important to understand accountabilities—where responsibilities start and end for each entity. Projects are delivered in segments; the sourcing partner has one and we have one. Each segment is evaluated and examined to see if we delivered on our respective commitments—a little different than before, but it is now our new norm.

Although a challenging experience, I did learn how to work with my remote team, and to trust my project manager, even though she was living many miles from me. I also sharpened my phone meeting skills and my ability to work with someone that I had never met in person. Over time, we shifted from a corporate culture where face-to-face meetings were essential to a culture where many different communication channels were the norm, and more acceptable.

We started to see real benefits when we began to work together to solve issues that were a challenge or unsolvable in the previous environment. The possibility of a flexible workforce seemed to be attainable. As we became better at partnering with teammates remotely, we were also able to leverage a larger workforce than ever before that could help ramp up projects quicker than we had in the past.

Our growing pains started to lessen over time, and the true value of the relationship started to unfold. I was able to sharpen my skill sets and be exposed to new ways of working. I am now able to have a meeting either in person or via conference call with similar results. Although I must admit, I do enjoy people contact, but I see the value of working remotely. I have also benefitted personally from leveraging remote work; I am able to work from home effectively, and enjoy the quiet when I have work that needs concentration. I have been able to see where the sourcing partner has strengths above and beyond what was here before, and was willing to share its talent and knowledge to make our workplace better. My company is more resilient, and we are better able to leverage talent in other areas of the country.

Although the decision to source may be a strange, winding, and sometimes frustrating road, it can get you to a better place than where you started if you are in it for the right reasons. My best advice is to go into a new sourcing arrangement with an open mind—the only thing that is certain is that it will not be what you think. Be willing to listen to your new sourcing partner, and to learn new skills. My company does a lot of things the "right way," but sourcing partners have experience to leverage that helped us through our own blind spots. Be open to different work cultures and different ways to get to the same goal. Finally, it is beneficial to remember that everyone is still one team, even if it is an extended team. This will help you to get the best out of the new situation, and your new partners will have the best chance to help you succeed, as you walk to your next destination together.

2.3 REDUCE COST: SHARED SERVICES

Companies are looking to gain economies of scale and increased productivity by creating shared service organizations to centralize roles that have common skills and attributes. As Figure 2.2 highlights, a shared service organization takes employees of similar skills out of dedicated teams and organizations and groups them together.

The shared services approach is predicated on a model of resources working on multiple similar activities being cheaper and more effective than having them working separately in different areas. The benefits include:

- Increased productivity due to pooling of resources with similar expertise so that work can be shared across the team.

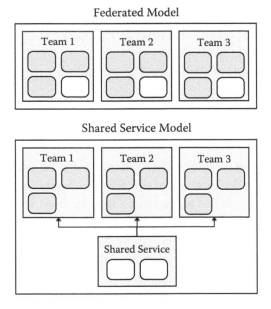

FIGURE 2.2
Standard shared services model.

- Better coverage for customers, as one worker can be used when another worker is not in the office or gets pulled for a different project.
- Lower operating costs due to a reduction in redundant management, redundant infrastructure, and overhead costs.
- Streamlined and consistent work across the shared domain because of standard processes used.
- Better outcomes as a result of sharing of knowledge and expertise between members of the shared service organization.
- Predictability in meeting commitments. Service level agreements (SLAs) or operating level agreements (OLAs) are documented that outline response times and commitments to customers.
- Minimized impact from losing key resources because the work is shared across many people within the shared organization.
- Scalable and flexible model as the workload and priorities change because the pool can be reassigned to different work quickly.

Shared service organizations are optimal for roles that are transaction based with a specific set of skills that don't require much specialization within a specific business area. There are several common examples of shared service organizations within information technology:

- Infrastructure services such as network support, the technology help desk, and desktop support
- Database administrators
- Training resources
- Quality assurance resources
- Customer help desk

When companies organize their shared services divisions they will sometimes look at the location of the division. Some organizations go so far as to centralize shared services in a new location that may pay lower wages than the current one. This is called a greenfield location—when that facility is in location where the company does not already have a presence. Keeping a shared service organization within an existing corporate location such as the corporate headquarters is considered a brownfield location. Most organizations use a brownfield approach because the facilities and infrastructure are already in place and there are no significant additional facility costs.

In order to fulfill the value proposition of cost savings and consistency of work, shared service organizations fractionalize resources and spread them across several concurrent activities and also create additional process steps. Resource fractionalization results in additional coordination for the project manager to manage the part-time resources, make sure they are ready when needed, and ensure that the correct skill sets are available for the project needs. The additional steps and processes need to be planned for as well.

2.3.1 Competing Priorities

For the realization of economies of scale benefits, shared service organizations usually promote a model of having their resources work on many concurrent activities and projects. Since the resources do not directly report to the project manager and usually have several competing priorities (i.e., other projects), it becomes a challenge for the project manager to manage the activities and dependencies on the project plan. From the perspective of the employees in the shared services organization, they may have three or four different project managers all pushing for their activities, each of which is identified as the highest priority. The project manager must have a flexible plan and allow enough lead time in the plan to account for the possibility that the resource is on other work. The project manager also needs to be cognizant of when to escalate expected slippage. Sometimes there is a challenge of knowing who to go to when there needs to be an escalation.

2.3.2 Additional Steps

In order to ensure standards and consistency of work, shared service organizations may introduce additional process steps and forms that are required for using their services. This usually means additional planning (and often paperwork) before the work can be initiated, as well as additional process steps to get the work done. For example, most infrastructure divisions are adopting the IT Infrastructure Library (ITIL) standards that identify all work requests as service requests. This usually requires the submission of a request, review of the request, routing of it to the appropriate team, prioritization of the work, and then scheduling of the work. All of this takes time to process before the work can even be started, which the project manager must account for in the plan and schedule. Then there are those items that the project manager may not even be aware of. For example, if a project manager isn't aware of a particular step, process, or form, that may put the entire project at a stop while those activities get completed.

2.3.3 Resource Skills

By centralizing resources and oftentimes using a "whoever is available" resource modeling approach, the project manager and project team run the risk of having a resource from the shared services area that may not have the right experience that the project needs. For example, if a tester has spent the last four years in the billing area working on billing systems, he or she has become familiar with the nuances of those particular systems. In a shared services model, the project team runs the risk of that expert billing system tester already on another critical project, and they get a new tester who is unfamiliar with those specific systems is assigned. Thus, the project manager, when working with the resource manager of such a shared service organization, must make very clear the specific resource type and skills that are being requested. Of course, the earlier the conversation and specific skill request takes place, the better the chances of acquiring the right resource. There is still always the risk of not getting the right resource and having to plan around that, which may mean waiting for someone to free up or extending the timeline to get someone up to speed.

2.3.4 Intangibles

Most shared services organizations centralize the resources in the same location for the sharing of knowledge and workloads. This usually means that the shared resources do not sit with the project team (even more so if the shared services group is at an off-site location), resulting in resources being less available for *ad hoc* questions and meetings than if they were sitting with the team. This is exacerbated by the many assignments that the resource is given. Usually what happens is that all of the project managers want the strong contributors, who then get overallocated to projects. There are also oftentimes higher-priority activities that come up and take resources away from project work. This requires the project manager to be extra diligent with shared service work to understand the risks and upcoming milestones.

Case Study: Three Scenarios for Working with Shared Service Organizations

Contributed by Rob DeLaubell

I am a project manager responsible for managing two information technology (IT) work streams that are part of an overall $100 million program spanning multiple years. Project management within my organization requires working in a highly matrixed environment, and leveraging resources that are part of shared services organizations.

As part of a Fortune 500 financial service company, and especially given the economic impact of the current recession, controlling costs are a driving factor in organizational structure. The following case discusses how project management within the program had challenges based on the trend of leveraging shared service organizations, the resulting impact, and commentary regarding the pros and cons of leveraging shared services.

Wikipedia defines shared services as "the provision of a service by one part of an organization or group where that service had previously been found in more than one part of the organization or group. Thus, the funding and resourcing of the service is shared and the providing department effectively becomes an internal service provider. The key is the idea of 'sharing' within an organization or group." There are three primary shared services organizations in my company that I interface within the course of IT software development: database administrators, the architects within the chief technology office (CTO) organization, and middleware service architecture and support.

SCENARIO 1—DATABASE ADMINISTRATION ENGAGEMENT

One specific example is engagement of database administrators (DBAs), which are now part of a central technology platform organization. Prior to our organizing DBAs as shared services, they were part of the organization that they supported. There was a relationship with a specific, single individual whom a project team could interact with during design, development, testing, and release of a project. The DBA had intimate knowledge of the applications that he or she supported, and engaging the DBA for support was as simple as stopping by his or her desk and making a verbal request. Cycle time for requests was relatively quick, and confidence in the quality of work was high, given the specialization that the DBA had developed. Now, engaging a DBA requires engaging the services of the platform organization. Aside from the extra administrative mechanics necessary in order to engage these services (such as opening a work request within our browser-based workflow system, or sending an e-mail stating the request to a distribution list of DBAs), the quality of service provided completely meets expectations.

The pros of using a shared services structure for DBA support are obvious: cost savings and scalability. The organization has been highly successful in realizing this financial benefit. And, the quality of services provided is solid (in many instances, it is the same individual resources that are doing the work that were previously part of the organization prior to the shared services model). Project managers can allocate DBA need fractionally using our resource demand system (in 5% increments), so that a particular project may request only the allocation that is needed for a particular project. On the con side, the processes that have been instituted around the engagement of DBAs require additional formality. For example, a DBA request may require submitting a form, and include specifics around business need, delivery requested date, and how to test (which may be more obvious to immediate project team members). The DBAs are not physically located with the project teams, requiring phone conversations, teleconferences, and e-mail exchange vs. face-to-face discussions more often than not. An additional point for consideration, on the con side, is that project teams may be somewhat limited in their ability to implement alternative methodologies, such as agile development, given that that the project manager has defined processes to follow when interfacing with the shared resources organization.

SCENARIO 2—ARCHITECT ENGAGEMENT

I consider enterprise architects as part of our CTO organization to be a shared service—perhaps somewhat stretching the definition. The shared service model we have for architects on my project is highly effective and working well. Specifically, we have a full-time CTO architect assigned to the project, and he is full-time physically present, co-located with the project team, and able to engage as necessary without the overhead as I described above. As a full-time member of the project team (although administratively aligned with a different organization), he is intimately tuned in to project details, and engages in design and development sessions as would any other team member. In addition, the shared services model for architects within my company enables my project to effectively scale when the need arises for additional architecture capacity (such as a need for a 50% resource for a three-month period). An additional benefit of having an architect 100% allocated is that the assigned CTO architect is able to be an advocate for the project team during the various architectural governance gates, sign-offs, etc. The architect, being part of the design team, is well positioned to socialize the designs among the architectural community. Well-defined roles and responsibilities have helped to proactively alleviate issues around accountability between the project team and the CTO organization.

SCENARIO 3—MIDDLEWARE SERVICES

My project team leverages the services of another shared service organization. Specifically, we utilize this team for technical expertise with technical middleware transformation products. Again, the shared services model is highly effective in this area, considering the technical nature of these products, and given that the project need for resources in this space is limited. My need for a technical resource, for example, is from 5 to 10% of an Full Time Equivalent (FTE), on average, over the course of a year. There are peaks and valleys of resource demand within any given project phase, such as initial deployments, which may require a 100% allocation of a resource for several days. Other periods of nonactivity may require no support on any given week.

COMPETING PRIORITIES

I recall receiving a telephone call one afternoon from a manager in one of the shared service organizations that supports our mainframe source code version control tools, advising that due to a production environment crisis in another area, work that was under way in support of a tool enhancement for my project would be temporarily suspended. Accordingly, they would not be able to deliver the enhancement on the previously agreed upon date. The enhancement he was referring to was very important to our development team (50+ developers), as it would simplify a time-consuming, manual process, and thereby better enable us to meet our aggressive delivery schedule.

However, production environment stability and availability trumps all other IT activities. Accordingly, I responded, "I understand. Please let me know what I can do to help." Generally speaking, my project, given its size, receives its fair share of support from the shared services area. In this case, the production incident exemplifies how competing priorities within the shared services area negatively impacted my project. Whereas the prioritization adversely impacted my project, it is important to note that priority was correctly focused from an organizational perspective.

CONCLUSION

Challenges abound working as an IT project manager within my organization. Schedules are aggressive, availability of subject matter experts (SMEs) are at a premium, and limited capital dollars for investing in IT work are continuously under scrutiny. The key to being an effective and successful project manager is to maximize the efforts and energies of all of my project team members, including those of our internal shared services organizations. Overall, I believe that my organization's shared services structure does provide me with the support that I need and is "right" for my organization.

2.4 INCREASED COMPLEXITY: MORE TECHNOLOGY LAYERS

Over the last thirty years the technology landscape has evolved significantly. In the 1980s most technology sat on a mainframe computer with "dumb" terminals and was pretty self-sufficient. During the 1990s client-server technology evolved where there was now a server that connected via a network to many client locations (e.g., personal computers). Figure 2.3 shows a simple relationship from a server to multiple clients via a network.

This client-server architecture then gave rise to the Internet architecture, where the "clients" were people's home computers connecting to Web servers. As the Internet evolved, so did the concept of separating specific pieces of the technology infrastructure into different layers that could be easily replaced and maintained. A classic tiered environment is shown in Figure 2.4, where components are organized across a presentation layer to display information, workflow layer to manage the activities, business logic layer to store the specific functions, and data layer to manage information.

Today there are many separate layers and technologies to consider when working on an IT project, including:

- Front end (presentation layer), which can include a Web page or portal technologies. There is also the validation of information that gets entered.

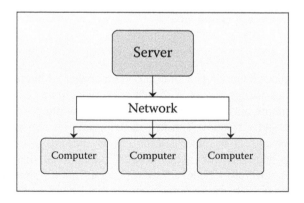

FIGURE 2.3
Client-server model.

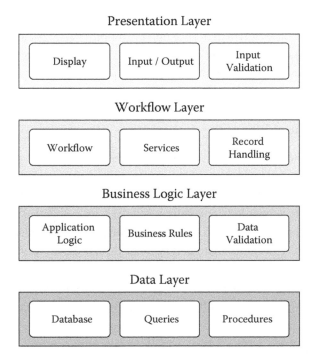

FIGURE 2.4
Example of a multitiered technical environment.

- Content and document management systems to access, tag, and house business content and documents.
- Security to manage the authentication and authorization of users.
- Business rules as a separate entity to store and manage the rules that govern business decisions.
- Integration layer to manage the integration between systems.
- Workflow to manage the user navigation through a business process.
- Data translation to convert data between several data stores.
- Data storage to house information and the ability to search and report on that information.
- Infrastructure, which gets broken down into several layers. A classic Internet application has a Web server, an application server, and a data server.

Each layer and component needs specific requirements, has to be designed for, and has to be built to specification. This includes considerations for the planning and integration of all of the components together.

With companies becoming more reliant on technology for big solutions, and that technology infrastructure becoming more complicated, the complexity of projects also grew exponentially. This poses challenges to the project managers in the form of additional planning needs and the need for specialized resources.

2.4.1 Additional Planning

With a multilayer technology comes the need for additional planning. For example, there are technology environments and software that need to be procured, set up, and managed. Usually these require working with procurement, outside vendors, and infrastructure services that all have process steps and lead times that need to be accounted for. There is also integration between the components that need to be designed, built, and tested.

All of these items result in more detailed requirements needing to be gathered up front and a more complex technical solution needing to be designed and built. As a result, there are many additional activities added to the project plan and an increased risk to the project due to having many integration points, technologies, and platforms that can fail.

2.4.2 Different Skill Needs

Separating the technology layers causes each layer to become specialized on a particular domain. The challenge with this is that now each technology requires specialized resources to perform the work needed to design, build, and test the component. Usually these resources come at a premium cost because of their specialized skills. There is also the challenge of finding the right resources who can integrate the different technologies and who understand enough of each component to ensure they fit together properly. These resources need to be planned for in advance (especially if they are outside contractors) and their cost needs to be included in the cost of the project.

Oftentimes, the project manager will need to account for a small team of resources from a particular area. Larger companies have numerous systems that handle their core processes. It is not uncommon to have a core mainframe system using multiple interface channels to other ancillary systems (e.g., billing, sales, marketing, reporting). When working on a project it is critical for the project manager to work with the technical leads to understand which specific systems may have an impact. Once that list has been created, the project manager then needs to reach out to those specific teams to understand the effort and resources required.

The project team may consist of a technical lead, a developer, a business analyst, and maybe even another project or resource manager from the impacted systems. To correctly plan, manage, budget, and coordinate, it is critical that during the early stages of a project the project manager plans accordingly for all facets of the impacted systems.

Because many project managers don't have a deep technical background, managing projects with many technical layers and newer technology is a key concern. There is a saying that "you can't control what you don't know." Therefore, having the right resources, even if they are more expensive, is important to success.

Case Study: Too Many Tiers Caused Too Many Tears

Contributed by Kerry Wills

I took over as the program manager for a $17 million program when it was in the build phase and already more than one year under way. As I got up to speed on the program, I quickly saw the intricate complexity of the technical solution being developed. The solution consisted of many different technology layers (or tiers).

THE TIERS

- Front end—A Web application was being built using a company standard portal technology, Web severs, and Java programming being completed by an offshore company.
- Business models—Behind the front end were business models that had specific rules that were used based on information entered into the front end.
- Services—The Web application also called on Web services to process information. There were three types of Web services that we used:
  - Internally developed Web services maintained by a team working for our organization
  - Vendor Web services that we purchased and maintained on site
  - Third-party Web services that were stored outside of our company that we "called" from our application
- Integration—We had to integrate our application with other applications to share information and used an integration layer to do this.
- Data mart—We aggregated several existing data warehouses and data marts into one. This required using translation technology to map and translate one data element to another data element.
- Reports—We ran reports off of the data mart for business users on specific information request.

THE TEARS

There were several hardships (or tears) of this complex technical design, which were evident as I started to uncover some of the problems on the program. These different layers required a lot of planning and coordination, and there was also difficulty in technically connecting the pieces.

First, there were many moving parts that needed to be planned for and coordinated. The technologies all had work to do within themselves, but also required integration with other technologies that needed to be coordinated so that they were ready at the right times. This required taking the project plans to the next level of detail. They were not at a level that could be managed to show the dependencies and impacts of slippage. For example, we ran into issues with one of the service vendors when its expected product release got delayed. The project plan was built around the assumption that this product would be ready on the original date, and we then had to scramble to understand the impacts and options.

There was also difficulty in technically connecting the pieces. When I first started on the program I polled the team for issues and decisions that needed to be made, and there were several technical issues with the integration of the components. For example, the standard portal technology being used did not fit well within the application architecture or services. The developers were also having a hard time reconciling some of the Java technologies with some of the services and other technologies.

DRY YOUR TEARS

I had several immediate priorities as I started to restructure the program. I needed to make sure that the plan accounted for the extra coordination and dependencies, ensure that the technologies used were the right ones for our program, and make sure we had the right resources to work with the technologies.

The first activity was to create the detailed project plans that accounted for the dependencies between the technical components and highlighted any risks. This required reviewing the technical designs and understanding what components relied on other components. From doing this we could make sure that the sequences in the plan were correct and that we understood which activities were on the critical path.

I then looked at the issues identified by the developers. In some cases, instead of asking the technical team what the options were to make the technologies work, I went back to the business stakeholders. I asked them how important some of their requirements were to the solution and made them aware that these requirements had complex technical components with the recurring cost of software licenses. It turned out that some of these requirements were "nice to have," so in the first two months I was on the project we eliminated four technologies from our design. This helped to simplify the solution. This probably also saved the company money in licenses, infrastructure costs, and resources needed to maintain the technologies after the project was finished.

Lastly, I looked to make sure that we were staffed with the right technical resources for each layer, and that they were coordinating properly. In some cases we had the resources on the team and in other cases we had to rely on our vendor partners.

CONCLUSIONS

There are several takeaways that I learned from managing this program around the use of complex technologies. First was the amount of planning and coordination needed. This includes the time to design the solution, prototype components, integrate the technologies, test the integration, and work with vendors. The other major lesson I learned was to make sure that every component is absolutely critical to adding business value. This is the classic "not wanting to use technology for technology's sake" line.

2.5 INCREASED COMPLEXITY: ENTERPRISE FOCUS

Many larger companies that have been around for more than a few decades most likely have had a history of buying technology to suit a particular division or project need without much consideration for what other technologies already existed at the company. This has led to companies having a large inventory of technologies, some of which perform redundant functions. Companies are now moving in a direction of determining standards at their enterprise level and looking to rationalize their technology inventories, which cost a lot of money to maintain and support.

The service-oriented architecture (SOA) strategy is founded on the approach of one piece of code, or service, providing one function for an organization, instead of creating and maintaining redundant functions. SOA separates functions into distinct units, or services, which developers make accessible over a network so that users can combine and reuse them in the production of applications (Erl, 2005).

In addition to creating services to perform unique functions, companies are also identifying standard vendors for specific technology domains. For example, they may identify Company A for the standard business rules engine, Company B for workflow, and Company C for the database

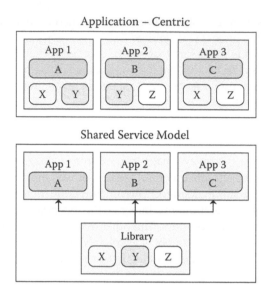

FIGURE 2.5
Application-centric approach vs. an enterprise focus.

platform. All projects using those technologies will be obligated to use those standard vendors, or make a strong case as to why they won't use them.

The result of services and standard vendors can be seen in Figure 2.5. In an application-centric approach, each application has its specific code (A, B, and C), but may also have the exact same functions (X, Y, and Z), which are now stored in multiple places. For example, both application 1 and application 2 have function Y in them. The enterprise focus model takes these redundant functions and moves them external to the applications in a shared library to be accessed. Some of these shared assets can also use standard vendors.

Having enterprise standards for services or vendors helps to keep the total cost of technology down and reduce redundancy, but it does pose some challenges to project managers. The standards being used may not be the best fit for the project needs, and projects may now have to build solutions that have more functionality than required by their business so components can be used as an enterprise standard.

2.5.1 Standards and Fit

Standards are usually declared to cover a broad range of requirements, and therefore, by using declared technology standards, a project may need to incorporate a technology that doesn't best fit the need of the project. This may result in additional effort to make it work within the environment of the project. In the end, this may add more cost and time than having created the component internally.

Project managers must work with their technical teams to understand when they need to take an enterprise focus with their solution, as well as when to use company standards and what the risks are for each option. These then need to be weighed against project goals and managed with the sponsors of the project.

2.5.2 Broader Requirements

Having an enterprise focus means that projects engaging in new technologies may need to understand broader requirements than just their particular scope. For example, a project has requirements to build a service that stores a client's name and address. In order to make this an enterprise service, the project team may have to build in the capability to also store the client's phone number, social security number, and employer address. These are additional requirements to the project outside of what the project stakeholders asked for, which the project now needs to plan for and build.

Like in the example, projects may need to facilitate requirements from stakeholders outside their project, which will add time to the schedule. It also means that the project will need to build functionality beyond the scope of what was asked for by its requirements, which also would add to the schedule and cost. This sometimes means that the project manager then becomes the salesperson for the enterprise capabilities to convince stakeholders to invest.

Another challenge for projects is facilitating who will pay for those changes, since the original project did not ask for the larger scope. These discussions should take place early on in the project to ensure that the chosen project direction is in alignment with the technical strategies of the organization. Some companies do have investment pools that they can use to supplement project budgets when reusable assets are created.

Case Study: Being Compliant Meant Being Complex

Contributed by Kerry Wills

In my consulting days, I was running a project for a large corporation that was developing a Web-based application. The design of this application had some workflow and external services built in to facilitate the user's progress through a predefined set of steps. At the time, the corporation had created a set of enterprise standards for using certain technologies, and the front-end portal software was one of them. The chief technology officer made a statement that all projects would use these standards. There was also a company-wide push to create enterprise services, which are technology components that can be reused on other projects. The project described in this case had impacts from both using standards and creating services that could be leveraged beyond the project.

FRONT END

Because the standard for the front-end technology had been set while the project was already under way, we had to refactor the application to fit it into the new front-end technology. We found several challenges when we did this. For one, the workflows and screens that we were using were incongruent with the technology, which meant that we had to change the way that the application worked. This meant that to meet the standard, we had to modify the design of the application, which resulted in rework and not meeting some of the business requirements because the technology standard could not support them. We also had to modify some of the code within the front-end technology to fit with other requirements that we had. Changing this code really meant that we weren't using the standard as it was set, but we would not have met our project commitments if we didn't.

Ultimately, we were able to incorporate the standard, but the net result was an increase in the complexity of our application. We had an additional layer by using the software product, and we changed the code base of it to meet our project requirements, thus making it more complex and difficult to maintain downstream.

SERVICES

We were also building some external services that would be called by the application for specific business functions. With the new focus on leveraging these services across the company, we had to facilitate requirements from other business areas and other projects. This added time and cost to our project to build additional functionality beyond our specific project requirements. While this was the right thing to do for the company, it had impacts on our project that we had to absorb.

The other challenge posed by creating these enterprise services was that there were projects who wanted to use them and had commitment dates before our project was supposed to be finished. This meant that team members from my project were essentially working to meet other project commitments and spending time supporting these services, which was not accounted for in my project plan.

SUMMARY

Having an enterprise focus on standards and the creation of reusable components makes a lot of sense for a company. However, as noted in this case, the impacts need to be considered and planned for. In our case, using the standard for the front-end technology and creating services with requirements beyond our own added extra time, cost, and complexity to our project that were not originally estimated or planned for.

2.6 INCREASED COMPLEXITY: THIRD-PARTY VENDORS

As technology has become more complex and specialized, the marketplace has flooded with vendors who offer solutions for specific business functionalities. Companies are also recognizing that they are not in the business of creating IT assets and want to leverage existing technologies from vendors that have proven them already. Instead of building their own custom technology solutions, companies are trending toward purchasing them. This can allow a strategy of using "best of breed" components from vendors to supplement a company's proprietary systems. The result is that most companies today have many different vendor products in their technology stack.

There are many considerations when determining whether a company should build a solution or buy a solution. This is known as a build vs. buy analysis. Some of the considerations are outlined in Table 2.1.

TABLE 2.1

Buy vs. Build Comparison

When to Build	When to Buy
• If a solution is unique to a business or proprietary to the company • When no technology solution exists to meet the business need • If the company has adequate resources to build, maintain, and support the new asset	• If the solution is not unique and there is pressure to deliver quickly—reduced time to develop solution because the solution already exists and can be used quickly • Desire to keep maintenance costs low—maintenance of the code is usually part of the contract • Desire not to manage specialized skills in a particular technical domain; can contract with the vendor for support

There are now third-party solutions for almost every business function, domain, capability, and layer of technology. Therefore, almost all technology projects today have at least one external vendor product to integrate and design into their solution. While this does decrease development time and possibly overall costs, there are project management challenges that need to be recognized.

Using a third-party vendor has several implications on projects, which include additional planning up front as well as a loss of control over portions of the project. These need to be factored in during any build vs. buy analysis.

2.6.1 Planning

Determining to use a third-party solution for a project requires additional planning up front. First, there is the marketplace scan to determine which vendors can meet the functional requirements of the project. Then, the team analyzes them based on a set of criteria and culls down the full vendor list to a short list of possible vendors. The project team may need to send an official request for proposal (RFP) to the vendors to have them describe their product/solution and also to schedule a demonstration.

A typical vendor analysis includes a list of topics to gauge different facets of the solution, which are given weights according to the priority as determined by the project team. These categories can include adequacy of solution to business need, adequacy of integration within the technical environment and technical standards, and adequacy of solution to project requirements (cost, timeline, etc.). A subset of the project team needs to be coordinated to perform the vendor analysis, including sitting in all demonstrations, reviewing the products, and completing the analysis activities.

Once the vendor analysis is complete, the scores and costs will be compared against each other to make an informed recommendation to project stakeholders. It can take weeks or months to complete the vendor list, submit and receive back the RFPs, schedule the vendor visits, conduct the demonstrations, score them, call back the finalists, and sign the contracts. All of these steps need to be contemplated by the project manager when performing a vendor analysis.

Also, the project needs to determine any additional activities and cost required to integrate the third-party software. These activities are usually hard to estimate up front, as integration activities are always complicated.

2.6.2 Loss of Some Control

Having a third-party vendor solution also takes some control away from the project manager. While vendors usually have teams working on the projects, the projects can oftentimes become reliant on the release schedule of the vendor product, which may jeopardize the projects' delivery commitments.

Another challenge when using a third-party vendor is that its solutions aren't usually easily customizable. This may pose a challenge to the project teams working with them to find alternatives or workarounds for features that they require. This analysis should have been contemplated during the vendor analysis, but oftentimes doesn't really come to fruition until the product is actually available by the project team. Customizing the solutions may result in the product no longer being contractually supported by the vendor, and also being off of the upgrade path for future releases.

Lastly, when using third-party vendor solutions, sometimes there are defects with the code (especially with new products). This may sometimes mean waiting in a queue of other defects to be fixed and released, which may have an impact on project schedules. The project manager needs to ensure that when a vendor is used, there is a key point of contact who can work with the project team on higher-priority defects to ensure that they are being managed and coordinated.

Case Study: Going from Using an External Product to Owning It

Contributed by Kerry Wills

I was managing the program management office of a multi-million-dollar program for a national corporation. This was, at the time, the largest program in the division and the company. The program had several streams of work that spanned across the division, used several vendor products, external consultants, and contractors, and had many integration points.

USING AN EXTERNAL PRODUCT

When this program started, the n-tier technology trend was starting to take off and the program designed this into the solution. The solution included a Web layer, an application layer, and a data layer, which was new to this division, which primarily had client-server applications. The developers on the team were relatively new to Web programming, so the technical team had made the choice to pursue code generation software, which could help to automate the build of the solution.

After an analysis of software programs, one vendor was selected because it had the best solution for generating code in our environment. The program went through the appropriate procurement and contract steps, and soon we had the software in house. We then proceeded to train our developers on how to use the software and engrained it into our build processes. After almost one year of use, the team had become well versed in how to use the software, and while it was "clunky," it did seem to help us generate and maintain code quickly.

By the time the team had gotten to the point where they were experts in the product, the company that owned the software fell into some troubles and told us that they were going out of business. This posed significant challenges to our program because our software code was embedded in this product and could not be removed easily. After several conversations with the vendor, it proposed that we could purchase the source code to the product.

OWNING THE PRODUCT

We ultimately wound up purchasing the source code to this product because it was cheaper than refactoring all of our code with the program already under way. However, from a long-term perspective this was not the best option for the company. We all recognized that we did not want to be in the code maintenance business, but we had no choice given how far the program was in its life cycle.

The major lesson learned from this program was that we had to have a better gauge of the stability of the vendor company before contracting to use its products. It is probably also a good idea to determine the exit strategy of a vendor before moving too far down the build path.

2.7 ADDITIONAL RIGOR: DEMAND MANAGEMENT AND GOVERNANCE

As information technology projects and programs become more strategic and grow in cost and duration, companies are recognizing that they need to treat these projects as investments. To manage these investments properly, two mechanisms are being used: project demand management and project governance. The high-level process for these approaches is shown in Figure 2.6.

Demand management is the process of looking at all business requests for IT projects (demand) and deciding which ones are highest priority and should be worked on. Since technology is involved in most facets of business, and it is a constrained resource (people and dollars), it is important that companies prioritize the spend appropriately. Managing IT demand

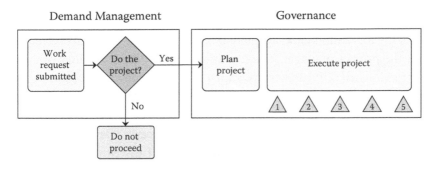

FIGURE 2.6
Project demand management and project governance.

usually involves several considerations, including existing spend and mix of projects in the portfolio, strategic alignment of projects, resource capacity to complete projects, and high-level estimates of costs and benefits to understand possible returns on investment. IT demand is usually managed via a committee of senior executives who review the request and prioritize it against specific criteria.

Because some of these investments won't yield returns for several years and also cost millions of dollars, companies are looking for ways to monitor the ability to realize the project benefits and to meet project commitments. Project governance is set up to have regular checkpoints at key points of the project. In Figure 2.6 these are seen as the numbered triangles below the project life cycle. For example, a checkpoint might be taken after an initial estimate is completed to see if the cost and benefit assumptions have changed as the project gets under way. If the project is degrading benefits or increasing costs, management may decide to stop it. Other checkpoints can happen after key stages in the project, such as requirements completion, build completion, and test completion. Usually these checkpoints involve stakeholders from the projects, sponsors, and even some people from outside of the project to provide an independent view into the health of the project and its ability to move to the next phase (phase containment). Checkpoints look at the progress of the project in its commitments (schedule, scope, and cost), as well as any key risks, issues, or resource needs. In some companies, funding is given out for each phase and the governance gates are used to get approval for funding and to continue working on the project.

Both demand management and governance are valuable tools for managing the investment of an IT delivery portfolio, but they do create new activities for the project managers to be aware of and manage appropriately.

2.7.1 Additional Planning

Preparing for demand management or governance gates requires attention from the project manager. Usually this means pulling together financial information, identifying what resource skills and effort are required, creating presentations, describing expectations around the timing of benefits, and reviewing that information with stakeholders to gain consensus on priority and commitments. Most likely these processes have special forms, checklists, or reports that need to prepared and distributed in advance. This process often requires a large lead time and heavy coordination from the project manager. These are all activities that need to be understood and included in the project plan.

Sometimes the governance process is set up in a way that the project cannot continue without getting approval on a specific phase of work. In these cases, the project manager needs to consider a plan for what happens if the project does not get approval to move on or requires additional activities before getting approval. This usually requires determining a plan for what to do with project resources (and their associated costs) while the activities are on hold or being redirected.

Governance also typically means building out a solid cost-benefit analysis (CBA) and presenting to management the rationale behind the project and the benefits to be gained. This process is typically labor-intensive and requires the project manager to ensure that the cost estimates are as inclusive as possible of all expenses, including labor, hardware, contingency, vendor, maintenance, licenses, etc. Oftentimes there are standard rates of return that need to be met in order for a project to be considered for approval. This requires the project manager to work closely with the project sponsors to ensure that the appropriate benefits are being quantified to outweigh the costs of the project. Governance planning should be baked into the project plan and planned for early enough in the process to create a positive story and increase the chance of governance approval.

2.7.2 No Slack

Because of the increased size and complexity of projects, there is much more scrutiny of them. Demand management and governance are both examples where management and other stakeholders are taking a closer look at projects and questioning timelines and cost. As a result of this scrutiny, there is sometimes a lack of appetite for any kind of slack on a project, whether that is schedule or additional cost. To some stakeholders, this looks like "fluff," which can be taken out as an easy way to reduce the project cost or schedule.

Schedule and cost contingency are levers that project managers traditionally used as ways of mitigating the risk of uncertainty and complexity. Today's projects are more complex and integrated than ever, so taking away this "slack" yields a tremendous risk to projects. On one hand, they are told to create estimates early on with little information, but then on the other hand, they are being held to those estimates without any mechanisms to manage the risk due to the complexity.

2.7.3 Intangibles

Because demand management and governance both require committees to approve funding and continuation of work, there are many stakeholders to work with. It can be difficult for a project manager to reconcile the different agendas of the people attending these meetings. For example, one stakeholder may not want to fund a project because he or she wants his or her project to be approved instead, and as a result may look to "poke holes" at the project being presented. A project manager should be aware of the organizational politics and leverage his or her sponsor in these discussions.

Case Study: The Impacts of Having Too Much Governance

Contributed by Kerry Wills

I worked in an organization that had just implemented a new governance process to control spending on information technology because the portfolio was growing into the hundreds of millions of dollars. At the time I was managing a project that was at the enterprise level, meaning it had implications that spanned across each of the four business segments within the company.

The governance process had several steps to it:

1. Each business segment had a governance meeting to review the proposed project. These meetings reviewed the scope of the project, benefits, and financials (cost-benefit analysis, internal rate of return, and break-even analysis). The attendees included the segment chief financial officer (CFO), segment project management office (PMO), and segment chief information officer (CIO). Project managers would then attend to present their projects at key points in the life cycle.
2. There was also an enterprise governance meeting to review projects that spanned several business segments. These meetings involved the same people as the business segment governance meetings, only these meetings had everyone in the room from all of the business segments.

3. There were technical governance meetings to ensure that the technical solution being proposed did not conflict with any corporate technology standards. These meetings were run by the architecture community.

The intent of the governance process made sense: to understand what the company was spending its money on, make sure that they are high-priority items, and approve the projects to move forward. However, there were many challenges that this caused, which were augmented on my project because it spanned several business segments.

AMOUNT OF TIME TO PREPARE

Because of the many governance meetings and different information required for those meetings, I spent a significant amount of time preparing slides and working with the finance team to create the financial information. Each governance meeting usually had a ten-slide presentation that outlined key project information, benefits, financial returns, and risks. While a lot of this information existed on the project, it still took time to organize it into the standard format and "massage" it for the meetings.

The governance process did not allow projects to move on until they got approval at the meetings. Therefore, if a project needed to go back for more information, it would have to wait several more weeks to present again to the governance meetings. This presented a dilemma with what to do with the project team members and also resulted in additional cost to hold them. To avoid this risk, I had premeetings set up with each key stakeholder at each of the segment governance meetings. This meant three or four people for each of the four business segments to ensure that they would support the project.

The time spent on preparing the presentations and premeetings was time that I was not spending running my project. Because of the different business segment meetings occurring at different times on the calendar, I felt like I was always either preparing for or attending a governance meeting.

DIFFERENT AGENDAS

Another challenge of the governance process was that different people attending the meetings had different agendas:

- The finance people wanted to see allocations of the project to their segment and returns.
- The PMOs wanted to see resource needs and risks.
- The business resources wanted to understand benefits and key capabilities that will be delivered with the project.

The difficulty with having people with these different agendas was that when the enterprise governance meeting occurred, any conflict could cause the project to not be approved or have to go back for more information. This meant a delay in the project and also starting the process over again!

CHALLENGES WITH RESOURCES

There was always the concern that if my project was not approved, then I would have to figure out what to do with the resources while I prepared for the next governance sessions. If I got rid of them, then I ran the risk of not being able to get them back on my project. However, if I kept them on the project, then I would incur a cost variance to cover them during time when they couldn't perform project work.

CONCLUSIONS

This case is not meant to bash governance processes. Governance is needed and important to managing a portfolio of projects. However, project managers need to recognize that there are impacts to governance processes and plan for them accordingly. Since this initial round of governance there have been several more evolutions to the governance process, which is much less disruptive to project managers today.

2.8 ADDITIONAL RIGOR: PROCESS AND TOOLS

As projects grow larger and more complex, the ability to consistently deliver on commitments across an organization becomes much harder. As a consequence, most companies have a standard set of delivery methodologies and tools that they use. There are also several existing frameworks for IT delivery in the marketplace today.

Methodologies typically include the areas illustrated in Figure 2.7. A standard framework shows the overall life cycle, which could be a waterfall model, agile model, or something else. Under the framework are standard phases that have specific procedures. These procedures then have activities and deliverables that need to be performed. Activities and deliverables can have guidelines for their use, checklists of activities to consider, and identification of which roles perform which activities. Deliverables can also have templates or high-quality examples that can be used.

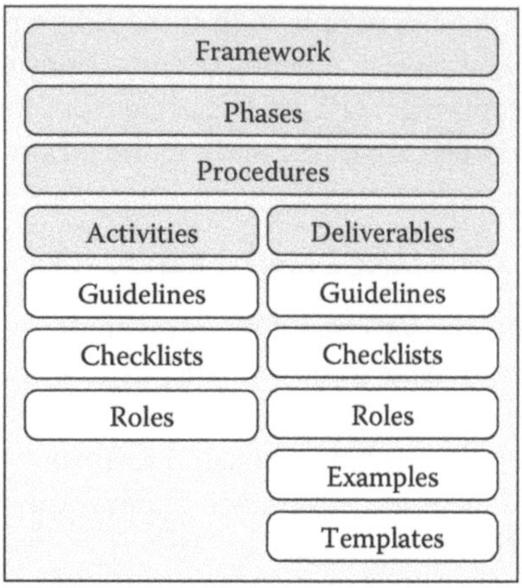

FIGURE 2.7
Typical components of a methodology.

Methodologies have many benefits, including:

- Standardizing delivery work and processes across an organization.
- Promoting reuse and consistency by providing guidelines, templates, and examples. By leveraging existing templates and examples, projects don't have to start from scratch each time.
- Clarity of project roles. Methodologies document project roles and their key responsibilities so that team members can understand the work that they are accountable for throughout the project life cycle.
- Consistency of tool usage. Some organizations tend to have a suite of different tools that are used at different points and by different resources across the project.

In addition to standard methodologies, companies are also using additional tools to help manage specific aspects of projects. Each of these tools requires setup, training of resources, and maintenance during the project. Some tools used on projects include:

- Project management tools to manage the schedule, activities, resources, status, issues, changes, and risks
- Portfolio management tools to manage portfolios of projects and monitor their health and progress

- Requirements management tools to manage requirements and their traceability throughout the project
- Quality management tools to manage test cases, test conditions, and defects
- Code management tools to manage versions of code

As projects become more complex, the usage of methodologies and tools has become pervasive on projects and has to be understood by project managers. In addition, there have been several regulatory initiatives over the last few years that have added processes for IT projects. For example, the Sarbanes–Oxley Act of 2002 (SOX) has specific regulations around document and information storage that need to be considered on projects.

These processes and tools are valuable for creating consistency in delivery, but they do increase the amount of work that project managers need to perform on their projects.

2.8.1 Additional Planning

Projects must plan for all of the delivery and other process activities. Some of these require significant planning time up front. For example, onboarding new resources may have a long lead time to acquire software and hardware for them, get them oriented, and get them access to certain systems. Methodologies include standard deliverables, reviews, and phase gates, which must be included in the project plan.

There is also planning involved in the use of the standard tools. This can include the time it takes to set up the tools, train project team members in the use of the tools, or additional steps required to use the tools properly.

2.8.2 Applicability

Standard processes and tools are created to be a guideline for most projects most of the time. Because of that, sometimes the deliverables don't always make sense for the project. For example, having a small project with a simple set of requirements fill out many detailed requirement documents may not be the best use of project resource time. Often there are multiple versions of a given template based on the size of the project. For example, there may be a full-blown requirements document with requirements traceability, or a smaller maintenance-sized requirements document where less documentation is required.

A project manager should understand his or her organization's tolerance for adherence to standards and work with the process organization to determine his or her approach for deliverables and tailoring, if allowed. If there is no tolerance for straying from the standards, then the project plan will need to account for all of these deliverables and activities.

Case Study: I Need Time to Process

Contributed by Kerry Wills

I have worked as a project manager in several Fortune 100 companies. They all have had methodologies for delivery and process steps to follow. One company that I worked for in particular seemed to have processes for everything, which I needed to follow in order to manage my projects.

This company had processes for many areas of the project:

- Software development—Steps to follow, standard deliverables, templates to fill out, and examples.
- Financials—Many different financial processes to follow, including creation of the CBA, tracking of project finances, and reporting.
- Procurement—Forms to fill out for ordering any software or hardware.
- Vendors management—Contracts and forms for working with vendors.
- Infrastructure—Steps and forms for any infrastructure service, including servers, releases, and desktop software installs.
- Human resources—There were processes to bring people on and also processes to roll them off.

The net result of these processes was that I spent a significant amount of my day working on these process steps, filling out forms, or redoing work because I did not follow something properly. There are a few examples where the many processes impeded my ability for the team to perform their activities.

The first example was when I had an outside contractor join the project as an assistant project manager to help me manage portions of the project. The person came on board, but we couldn't get her network access because the forms couldn't be filled out until she had an employee ID (which we couldn't get until she started). So we managed to find her an existing machine to work on and I was logging on with my ID. I was going away on vacation, so I gave her my password to log in to the computer, because her access was still not ready when I had to leave, and there was no other work that she could have done that did not require network access. Apparently while I was on vacation she was having problems with the computer and called the help desk, telling them that she was logged on as me. When I returned from vacation I had a voicemail from the threat management group (which I did not know existed until then) telling me that what I did was not proper. We sorted it all out and she eventually got access, but the process took almost two weeks, where we would have been paying this contractor and have had no way to make her productive.

The second process challenge that we had on this project was the many different forms and standards that needed to be used. We spent a significant amount of time working with the process organizations to make sure that everything was included in the project plan and that we did not forget any deliverables. Some of them were valuable, such as the requirement or testing approaches. Some of them did not make a lot of sense, but we included them anyway because they were standard documents.

From this project I gained the awareness and importance of understanding the processes so that they would not have a negative impact on the project. Since working on that project, one of my first activities on a project is to inventory all of the processes that may be used and make sure that they are accounted for in the estimate and the project plan. I have also not given out my network password to anyone since that project.

2.9 CHANGING WORKFORCE: SPECIALIZED RESOURCES

As a result of the increasing complexity of technologies and solutions needed to delivery on business strategies, project resources have started to become very specialized in the work that they do. There are two areas where resources are becoming more specialized: within a specific skill of project delivery and within a specific domain or technology. Table 2.2 gives examples for each area of specialization.

TABLE 2.2

Examples of Work Specialization within IT Delivery

Specialized Skills	Specialized Domain Expertise
• Business architects	• Business rule technologies
• Performance testing	• Content management technologies
• Component estimation	• Workflow technologies
• Technical solution design	• Front-end technologies
• Infrastructure planning	• Integration technologies
• Release management	• IT security
• Configuration management	• Reporting and metrics
• User-centered design	• Programming languages (e.g., Java, C++, .Net)
• Usability testing	

As resources become more specialized, project managers must make sure that they identify the appropriate resources that they require for the project, and ensure that they are lined up in time for when they are needed.

Having specialized resources on a project poses a few challenges to the project manager, which need to be considered when planning and running the project. Specialized resources tend to be in high demand (and low supply), which usually means they are more expensive and harder to find than other project resources. Also, because of their specialized focus, they tend to not understand the overall scope of the project, which puts the onus on the project manager to ensure the linkages between the components.

2.9.1 High-Demand Resources

Because specialized resources have deep skills in a particular area of project need, they are usually in high demand from many projects. There are a few considerations for working with these high-demand resources that a project manager must be aware of and consider in his or her planning:

- The skills are sometimes not available within the company and may require an outside contractor. This requires lead times to find a good fit for the project. It may also result in paying a higher rate for the contractor.
- They are usually expensive because they have deep skills that are not commodities and are in high demand.
- They are hard to obtain because there is a high demand for their services, and the project may end up with a fraction of the needed resource's available time, thus elongating the project schedule.
- There is always the risk of resources leaving because of the high demand for their work, and based on the nature of their skills, they are usually a critical resource on the team with no backup.

Project managers need to be aware of these risks and put in place mitigation activities, such as having other resources shadow the specialized resource or allowing for longer lead times for that resource to complete the task if he or she has fractionalized availability. Project managers must also consider the possibility of not getting the specialized resource and determining the plan for that scenario.

2.9.2 Missing the Big Picture

The other challenge with the specialization of resources is that it requires much more coordination at the project management and team lead level. As resources become more deeply focused on their own domains, the need increases for splitting out the work across these different specialty areas. It is not uncommon for a project today to have five or more architects working on it. For example, a system might need architects for the front end, business rules, workflow, content management, information, integration layer, security, and business functions. While these resources are well versed in their areas of expertise, there is now the additional need to ensure that there is coordination across those domains. In the example, this could mean having the front-end architect coordinate with content management, integration, security, and workflow functions.

Additional rigor is needed on the project to ensure that the specialized resources are onboard when needed, optimally engaged because of their cost and demand, and well coordinated so that the solution works when pieced together.

Case Study: A Tale of Two Experts

Contributed by Kerry Wills

I was working on a large multiyear and multi-million-dollar program that was creating a new Web-based system for a Fortune 100 company. The solution was to create a multitiered architecture with a Web front end for business users, an application server in the middle tier, and also an external rules engine to house all of the business rules, which could be modified by business resources.

As we started to plan for the project, we realized that we needed specialized resources to join the team; specifically, we needed experts in the rules technology and the application server technology. We did not have those skills on the team, and they were critical components to the solution that we were developing. Because these were specialized skill areas, it took us a long time to find capable resources. We received many resumes from people, but as we screened them and interviewed candidates, we found that most did not have enough experience with the technologies.

RULES EXPERT

We eventually found someone who was an expert in the technology that we were using. He was a contractor and was on another engagement at the time, so we had to wait some time for him to start. He eventually came on board and caught up in time to help us design the rules components properly. Luckily, we weren't too far into the requirements phase that we had to redo work based on the design approach.

Because this resource was in high demand, he wound up taking an assignment at another company midway through the project. This left our project in a scramble to find someone to replace him. We had existing team members who had been working with him long enough to pick up the work.

APPLICATION SERVER EXPERT

We couldn't find the right resource for the application server technology, so we wound up going with a professional service resource from the vendor of the technology. This resource cost us over $300 per hour on the project (not including his travel expenses), which was nearly four times more expensive than the other project team resources.

There were times on the project where the requirements were not completed or there were other delays that caused us not to leverage the expert to his fullest. I always had his rate in the back of my mind and tried to keep him as loaded up with work as possible, but there were definitely times that we were not getting our money's worth because we were not being effective with his time.

CONCLUSIONS

I learned a few lessons from this project about using specialized resources:

1. You need to plan for the time it will take to find capable resources and have a backup plan in case you don't get them in time.
2. Even when they join the project, have a backup plan in case they leave. This can include training existing team members by having them partner with the expert.
3. More diligence is required in planning for the activities of the experts because their rates are so high. Project managers should look to make optimal use of the time that the experts are working on the project.

2.10 CHANGING WORKFORCE: MOBILE RESOURCES

A prominent trend in the corporate workforce is that people have become more mobile, instead of staying with one company for a long period. Today, the concept of an employee working for the same company for his or her entire career seems to be folklore. In some places it is looked at as a bad thing—that an employee was stagnant in his or her career, as opposed to someone being loyal and dedicated.

There are several reasons for this trending lack of tenure:

- As a result of strategies such as outsourcing and the use of vendors for key project work, there may be a perception that companies are no longer committed to their own resources. As a result, people may not feel the same loyalty to companies as they once did, because they do not feel it is reciprocated.
- Resources are becoming experts in specific skills and technical areas that are transferable across different companies and industries. There is also high demand for specialized skills, causing people to leave their current employers for better opportunities, sign-on bonuses, and higher salaries.
- People may want to leave the corporate world and work for themselves, becoming independent consultants. The amount of red tape and process at a company may turn people away from wanting to work at a corporation.
- Changing needs for resources are forcing people to relocate and find new work. For example, when outsourcing was big with manufacturing companies, the resources being outsourced found work in financial companies, which were not yet outsourcing those skills. Now those financial companies are starting to outsource, so people are moving into other industries.
- Increased turnover in corporate management results in attrition due to changing strategies, new management decisions, reorganizations, and having loyalties to the old management team.
- Volatility in corporations and the economy is causing uncertainty and people to leave for safer industries or companies.
- The complexity and stress of the new environment result in people seeking new professions.
- Companies don't seem to place the same emphasis on morale as they used to. In the expense-cutting world that we now live in, people perceive themselves as being viewed as expenses and not necessarily as valuable assets. This diminishes morale and can result in higher turnover.
- New generations are entering the workforce. Generation X (born between 1965 and 1979) and Millennial (born after 1980) employees have a reputation of being self-focused, have a sense of entitlement, and do not have loyalty. Their values are different than those of older generations because of the prosperity and culture from their childhood.

Regardless of the reason for the mobile workforce, it is a reality that projects must consider. The chances of having a multiyear project retain the entire team for the entire duration of the project is very low. Therefore, a project manager must recognize this risk and plan accordingly.

There are many impacts that can result from losing key resources on a project, and all of them pose significant risk to the project's ability to meet its commitments.

2.10.1 Losing Key Resources Impacts Success

When any project resource leaves the team it causes a disruption. Losing key members of the project team can have significant impacts on the project. Several examples of these impacts include:

- Low morale. If the team member leaving was a well-liked resource that motivated the team and was seen as an informal leader, there could be a decrease in morale and team focus as a result.
- Project manager loses focus. Instead of focusing attention on managing the plan, issues, and risks, the project manager has the fire drill of addressing the resource gap and assessing the impact.
- It may be contagious. Sometimes when one team member leaves a project, others soon follow.
- Project commitment impacts. If the resource that is leaving the project team was on the critical path and has a hard-to-find skill set, then there will most likely be increases in the project schedule due to the delays in finding a replacement. Project cost may even increase because of the pushed schedule and inefficiencies of a new resource coming up the learning curve.
- Quality impacts. Quality may suffer when a new resource is brought in if he or she is unfamiliar with the environment and doesn't have the experience or knowledge of the previous employee. If the resource cannot be replaced easily or quickly, then the entire project may also be in jeopardy of being cancelled or delayed.
- Other project impacts. Sometimes when a project team member leaves and that project has a lot of visibility, the replacement is taken from another project. This can cause an impact to that secondary project, which is losing its resource.

Losing resource members is a reality in the current environment, and it needs to be recognized as a major risk to the project.

Case Study: Hard to Come By, Easy to Go

Contributed by Kerry Wills

I was running a large program for a company, and we were getting ready to kick off another project within the program and needed a lead business analyst to run the team of BAs. The project manager for that project and I spent several months on the process of obtaining this resource. First, we had to create an open job posting and look for qualified candidates within the company. When we did not find any internal candidates, we made an external job posting and looked for people outside of the company who would fit our requirements.

HARD TO COME BY

We interviewed many people over several weeks and eventually came across a solid business analyst who was working at another company at the time. We made her a job offer and, after a few days of consideration, she accepted it, but wanted to start a few weeks later. This was so that she could get her bonus from the other company and then join us (plus get our signing bonus as well). Because of the difficulty in finding qualified resources and the time that we had already spent, we agreed and started the project without her, assuming she would have to catch up on the work that was missed when she did start.

Once the resource joined the project team, we then had to get her acclimated to the project, the company, and our tools and processes. So she spent another few weeks attending orientation meetings, process training, tool training, and meeting with people from the organization to understand our work. Then there was the learning curve and getting up to speed on how to do things at our company. Eventually she had learned the work and was a very successful business analyst.

Over the course of the project she built strong relationships with the business stakeholders, learned the nuances of their business, understood the technical limitations of the technologies, and was very skilled at using our internal tool set. Unfortunately, our organization did not have a very strong community for business analysts, and we had many discussions over the course of the project about this void that she felt.

EASY TO GO

Less than one year into the project and her tenure with the company, this business analyst wound up accepting a new role at another company. There were several reasons for her departure:

- It was a promotional role for her
- She did not feel like she had a lot of organizational support within our company.
- It was closer to where she lived.

While we tried to counteroffer, she had made up her mind and was not willing to accept any other offers. The net result on the project was that we had invested one year in getting her oriented and building her skills, and that was all gone. We had to start over and get a new resource, while still trying to meet our original project commitments.

CONCLUSIONS

From this experience I learned the value of keeping good resources challenged, motivated, and committed to the project because of the investment it takes to get them onboard and up to speed. I also am more conscious of cross-training resources and setting up a backup strategy for the key players on the project team.

2.11 SUMMARY OF IMPACTS

Because of the trends outlined in the sections above, there are many impacts to the work that project managers must consider and plan for on their projects. These are summarized in Figure 2.8 in a "heat map" that shows the relative impact of each trend.

In aggregate, the project trends identified and listed in Figure 2.8 have four thematic impacts on project delivery:

1. Additional steps. Additional activities are required that the PM must manage. These require more planning up front to prepare for these activities. This is always challenging given the pressure from stakeholders to deliver quickly. However, these cannot be overlooked because any oversight can cause delays on a project and also have additional unplanned cost. For example, not obtaining approval on the right form may result in not having a vendor, consultant, or shared service resource available to work on the project when he or she is needed.

   These activities also require more time from a project manager during the project to ensure they get executed properly. This means that on top of the normal project delivery activities, a project manager now needs to work with other areas and ensure that these new steps are completed properly.

Impacts to Projects

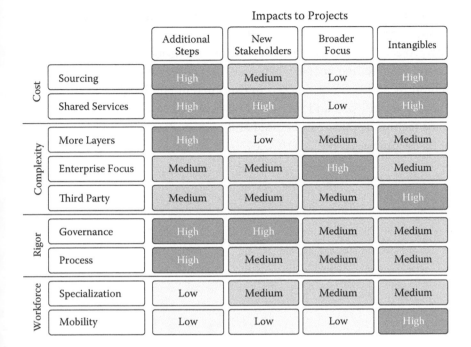

		Additional Steps	New Stakeholders	Broader Focus	Intangibles
Cost	Sourcing	High	Medium	Low	High
	Shared Services	High	High	Low	High
Complexity	More Layers	High	Low	Medium	Medium
	Enterprise Focus	Medium	Medium	High	Medium
	Third Party	Medium	Medium	Medium	High
Rigor	Governance	High	High	Medium	Medium
	Process	High	Medium	Medium	Medium
Workforce	Specialization	Low	Medium	Medium	Medium
	Mobility	Low	Low	Low	High

FIGURE 2.8
Summary of impacts of the project landscape.

2. New stakeholders. Today, there are many organizations and vendors involved in projects. These stakeholders need to be involved in the planning and management of the project. There is also the need for constant communication with them in order to successfully coordinate the work and manage expectations with them. This requires more coordination and relationship management from the project managers.

3. Broader focus. The focus of the project manager needs to be broader than just the specific project needs. Projects must now consider company standards and processes in their plans, and also bear the additional cost of them. Sometimes these add extra activities or requirements that weren't originally scoped into the project.

4. Intangibles. Other impacts (intangibles) need to be considered and managed, such as focusing on morale, cultural issues between employees and outside organizations, aligning resources appropriately, and job satisfaction. These require attention from the project manager, as they add risk to the project.

In order to effectively manage these new trends on projects and be successful, a project manager with a different set of skills and focus is required. The project manager of yesterday, whose main focus was on building a project plan, telling people what to do, and communicating status, is now behind us and will not succeed in this current challenging environment. These new skill sets and focus will be explored in Chapter 3, along with some techniques that can be used and case studies to highlight examples of the techniques.

3

The New Project Management Skills

3.1 OVERVIEW

The commonly used old model of "command and control" project management does not work in today's environment. In actuality, when used, that style of management tends to have the opposite of the intended effect on projects and team members. For example, a team with resources who are fractionalized and do not report directly to the project manager will not respond well to insensitively being told what to do and when to do it, and may even focus on other activities or projects before doing their work on that particular project. Without the proper influence, leadership, and motivation, team members will lose morale, focus on other work, produce lower-quality results, and possibly even leave the project.

Project manager skills need to evolve in response to the changing makeup of projects and organizations, as described in Chapter 2. Because the new project landscape requires more activities, has many interaction points, and has new stakeholders to manage with less direct influence, project managers need to have an updated set of critical skills and techniques in order to be successful. It is not enough today to know how to create a project plan or manage a risk log. There are four major categories of new skills: having additional rigor, taking a more consultative approach, having a deeper focus on information management, and using leadership skills to better influence and motivate people.

3.1.1 Additional Rigor

Because of the increased complexity, additional process steps, and additional stakeholders, more planning is required up front. This includes planning for additional activities, involving stakeholders early, obtaining commitments from different areas and resource managers, and setting proper expectations. There is also a need for additional diligence throughout the project to stay on top of its many moving parts. Examples include coordination with vendors, management of integrated activities, confirming resources are available when needed, change control analysis, and constant attention to the plan. Being organized, proactive, and diligent is essential to managing the project and understanding the progress toward the goals. Any slippage can have a domino effect on the project and cause schedule delays or additional cost if not managed properly.

3.1.2 Consultative Approach

Having rigor is foundational for understanding activities and managing the work, but project managers today need to be much more consultative than ever before. This is the biggest change in project management skills needed. In the past, project managers could just tell their teams to work harder or "make it happen" because they managed the entire plan and owned the resources. Since most resources today do not report to the project manager and are sometimes allocated to other activities, a project manager must rely on having good influencing and negotiation skills. There are also many more stakeholders who have involvement in the project who need to be worked with closely for successful outcomes. Being consultative includes building relationships early and utilizing them during the project, a focus on influencing others, and self-management.

3.1.3 Managing Information

The management of information is critical to the success of projects in the new landscape and is compounded with the many new stakeholders on the team. Communication includes internal messages to the team as well as external messages to the many organizations that need to stay apprised of the project status. These stakeholders can include the business, vendors, resource managers, related organizations, and team members on other projects in the portfolio. Communication is also an important vehicle for managing expectations and providing transparency regarding the health of the project. Communications need to be properly planned for, based on timely information, and presented in a way that the audience can understand the intended message.

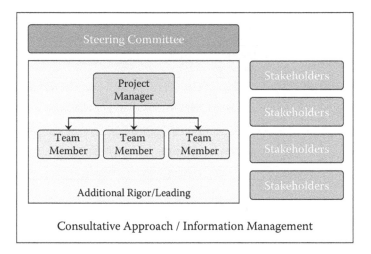

FIGURE 3.1
Critical skill sets for project management.

3.1.4 Leadership

The new project manager must be able to manage the work and lead a team of disparate people, some of whom do not report to the project manager or even work in the same country. Understanding what drives people and inspiring them to meet the goal is an important skill in being successful. This means knowing when and how to motivate team members to perform work, knowing when to empower them with key parts of the project, and being a champion for the team.

As Figure 3.1 illustrates, the project manager needs to focus on additional rigor and leadership within the team and then also be consultative and communicate throughout the entire project landscape.

Each of the four focus areas will be described in detail, with recommendations on best practices, techniques to use, and skills to build. They will also be supplemented with examples from real projects and practitioners to highlight cases where the skills and techniques were used successfully.

3.2 ADDITIONAL RIGOR

Project management has always been fundamentally about creating plans and executing them, while at the same time managing issues and risks as they arise. This nature tends to attract people to the profession who are

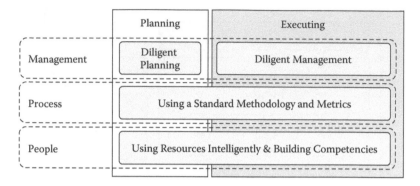

FIGURE 3.2
Rigor needed in planning and executing a project.

organized and diligent in following up on activities. In the new environment there are many more activities that the project manager must be aware of, plan for, and manage. Therefore, it is more critical than ever to be rigorous in all aspects of managing a project.

Figure 3.2 shows that attention is needed to planning and execution of the project across several domains:

- Management—Diligence throughout both the planning and execution of the project.
- Process—Using a standard methodology for delivery as well as key metrics to monitor the progress of the project.
- People—Using resources optimally and improving their competencies.

Project managers must be rigorous in all of these areas to be successful because anything not managed well in any of these areas can cause problems with the project.

There are several techniques that can be used to increase the rigor on projects, but the common theme with all of them is that they require proactive management and attention by the project manager. The following subsections will describe each of these techniques in detail.

3.2.1 Diligent Project Planning

Proper planning on projects is more important now than ever. The increased complexity of stakeholders, organizations, technologies, processes, and solutions requires that project managers spend the appropriate amount of time early on in a project. Because of the considerations made up front, planning has to be seen as an investment and not something to be rushed.

There are many important reasons to diligently plan the project:

- The commitments of the project (cost, benefits, schedule, resources, and scope) are determined in the planning phase. This includes making many assumptions based on available information. There must be a clear "contract" between business and IT so that there is consensus as to what is being delivered when and for how much, so that proper expectations can be set.
- The road map for the entire project is created during planning. This includes the project plan with key activities, deliverables, and milestones. It also includes the resources plan, which outlines what resources are needed, at what times, and where they will come from (employees, vendors, contractors, etc.).
- Rushing through planning activities can result in missed steps, unanticipated costs, and low quality.

Project managers need to set appropriate expectations with customers and management around the need to spend proper time planning in order to avoid additional cost, schedule slippage, and quality issues later. Project managers should also manage expectations around the assumptions made during planning and the confidence of the estimates based on known information. These are good examples of where influencing and the consultative approach described in Section 3.3 can be used.

The techniques outlined below describe the diligent activities needed to make sure that the project is properly planned.

3.2.1.1 Techniques and Skills

1. Technique—Plan to include the additional activities. As described in Chapter 2, there are many new activities introduced into projects that need to be understood and accounted for by the project manager when creating the initial project plan, resource plan, schedule, and cost estimate. Examples of these additional activities and considerations include:
   - Documentation needed for vendor or sourcing partners, such as access forms, contracts, and statements of work
   - Ramp-up time and knowledge transfer to outsourcing partner resources
   - Logistics for outsourcing partners and vendors, including access to systems and creating of network IDs

- Communications planning to all stakeholders
- Process activities such as required deliverables or deliverable reviews
- Governance gates and associated prework
- Process steps to obtain project resources from other organizations
- Forms to fill out for procurement
- Financial models to be maintained
- Overhead costs of management
- Lead times to obtain infrastructure, bring on and orient team members, prepare for governance gates, and sign vendor contracts

Creating a checklist is a great way for a project manager to list all of the affected areas, technologies, and stakeholders. The project manager can then reach out to all constituents to see what their required activities are and include them appropriately in the plans. Most organizations have checklists specific to their areas, and some even have checklists of considerations across their enterprise.

2. Technique—Plan for small units of work. Because of the trends mentioned in Chapter 2, projects are growing in complexity and size. As a result, milestones on projects are getting farther apart because of longer durations to deliver solutions. A project manager needs to have a clear pulse on the project work to gauge the ability to meet commitments. Therefore, it is a good practice to plan for small units of work that can be managed tightly.

There are many benefits to managing work in small units:

- Project managers can monitor the progress of the project and understand early when there are risks to schedule slippages or challenges. Having small units of work allows the project manager to tie the plan to the cost and schedule estimates, and therefore be able to quantify any slippage in dates to those commitments.
- Team members have frequent dates to work toward. Having milestones with long durations can sometime result in team members being lax because they think they have ample time to complete the work.
- Implications of changes can be assessed more easily. This can help the project manager communicate implications instead of being told to "absorb them" because the schedule appears to be long.
- Tracking time at a unit level allows project managers to understand how long each unit takes to design and deliver. This information can then be used to calibrate estimation models based on units of work.

In order to plan for small units of work, it is helpful to understand the taxonomy of a project plan. A typical project plan includes the following levels:

- Project—Overall collection of work, with a specific start and end date, that produces a desired business result.
- Phases—Discrete groupings of work with specific outcomes, such as requirements build and test.
- Milestones—Dates on the plan that mark the completion of a piece of work. Usually these are within the context of a phase and can include one deliverable or several integrated deliverables. Phases can also be milestones.
- Deliverables—Tangible object produced as the result of completing specific activities of work. Examples can include a requirements document, test cases, or a working technical component.
- Activities—Actions that project team members need to perform to complete an explicit deliverable.

The project manager should look at the project plan to determine the smallest units that can be managed and measured. Most projects monitor and report on phases and milestones. In order to track smaller units of work, project managers should also consider tracking deliverables, and possibly activities if the deliverables are long in duration. For example, a project can track the requirements deliverables as one milestone or break them into specific use cases or requirements packages.

Very diligent projects use a technique called earned value to manage discrete pieces of work. The concept of earned value is simple: projects "earn" work as it gets completed, which is then compared to their plans for work completed (also called "burn") to measure progress. Earned value requires that cost of work in progress gets calculated, which requires work to be broken down into small entities. While earned value takes some time to plan, it is very effective in helping a project manager to understand the progress. There is significant documentation and several tools in the marketplace that can help with earned value management.

3. Technique—Plan for rework. No project ever goes exactly as planned, although project managers always seem to plan and estimate as if they will. There is so much uncertainty up front on projects, but it seems that project managers are always asked for high-confidence estimates that account for everything, but then are not given flexibility

when assumptions are wrong or information is gained as the project progresses.

Also, the quality and productivity of project work completed are a function of the skills of the team and their familiarity with the business and technologies used. For example, a project using a new technology that has not been used before at the company or whose resources do not have a deep background in it will have some growing pains, which will most likely result in rework. This needs to be acknowledged and planned for.

There are two main techniques that can be used to mitigate the risk of not knowing a lot of information early on in the project and the chance of rework:

- Account for rework in the plan. For deliverables that are complicated or risky, rework should be put into the project plan. For example, if a project is changing the workflow of a specific business function into a completely new way of doing business, it should be expected that the requirements will be volatile as they are worked through. The first time a business customer sees the new requirements, they may want to modify things or realize that they missed key components. Without planning for this rework, a project manager will have to treat this as a change control, which will be a difficult conversation with the business customer who doesn't see this as a "change" in the requirements.

- Utilize contingency. Contingency is used on projects to account for unknowns early on when estimating project cost. Companies have complicated models, based on risk of the project, to calculate the amount of budget contingency to add to the estimate. For example, a moderate project costing $1 million might get an additional 20%, or $200,000, in budget as contingency to use.

Usually finances can be managed through resource utilization and other means, but schedule is much harder to manage to. Therefore, schedule contingency should be considered at key points in the project. This could mean adding one or two weeks at the end of requirements, design, build, and test phases. Sometimes projects rush toward the end of phases and don't meet the date, which causes poor quality, overlapping work, and rework. Having schedule contingency is an effective way of buffering the schedule to allow for unknown slippages. Project managers should be considerate as to not have both financial and schedule contingency and add too much buffer to the estimates.

4. Technique—Define and document the project management approach. Early in a project, it is helpful to define and document the approach for managing the different operational components of the project. Most standard delivery methodologies have a project management approach or charter deliverable to document these. The format or template does not matter so much as the fact that the project manager plans and communicates how the project will be managed. Table 3.1 lists common areas of operational focus in a project management approach.

Spending the time to plan a good approach to the project operations will help the project manager handle any challenge that arises because he or she has mechanisms in place to manage it. Documenting the approach also provides clarity of expectations to the team, so these should be shared with the project team at the project's kickoff.

TABLE 3.1

Project Management Approach Considerations

Area	Description of Approach
Plan management	How the project plan will be created, maintained, and tracked; also includes the approach for integration with subplans
Schedule management	How the schedule and milestones will be tracked and communicated to stakeholders
Resource management	How resources will be tracked, including on-boarding and off-boarding
Budget management	How the project financials will be forecasted, tracked, and reported
Action item management	How action items will be identified, assigned, tracked, and managed
Issues management	How issues will be collected, analyzed for impact, and escalated to management
Risk management	How risks will be identified, assessed for impact, acted on, and communicated
Decision management	How decisions will be made and documented
Communication management	How communications will be managed, including meetings and information distribution
Document management	How project files will be stored and version controlled
Scope management	How scope will be managed, along with the process for assessing and deciding on change controls

5. Technique—Set up a project management office (PMO). To assist in running the operations of a project, a project manager should consider setting up a project management office (PMO). This is a part of the project management function that serves to manage the operational components of a project. These are typically used on large projects where there are a lot of moving parts to manage.

A standard project management office manages the following aspects of a project:

- Plan management—Tracking completion of activities, reporting on progress, and looking at upcoming activities.
- Resource management—Coordinating the forecasting, on-boarding, and off-boarding of project resources.
- Financial management—Analyzing and reporting on cost tracking and forecasting.
- Scope management—Administering the change control log and coordinating the impact assessment of proposed changes.
- Issue and risk management—Aggregating issues and risks, reporting on them, and helping to see them to closure.
- Vendor management—Working with procurement to oversee contract creation and compliance to commitments.
- Communication management—Collecting status, preparing presentations, and reporting to the various stakeholders.
- Document management—Coordinating the storing and sharing of project information.

There are many benefits to having a PMO:

- Allows the project manager to focus on running the project. Having a team of people analyzing the project information supports the project manager in focusing on running the project.
- Dedicated focus. A team of people focused on the project operations can be diligent in gathering and analyzing project information, including looking ahead at the plan to make sure the project is ready. They also help to coordinate the many moving parts of a project.

While there is a cost associated with having additional resources to manage a PMO, the complexities of projects make a PMO essential.

6. Technique—Understand history of similar projects. Historical project information can be extremely helpful when planning a new project. Often, though, projects view themselves as unique and therefore don't look at lessons and documents from prior projects. However,

understanding similar projects can help the project manager in many ways:

- The project plan can be used to understand stakeholders, key activities, and durations for activities.
- Final project financials and resource plans can help with estimating the cost and resources for the new project.
- Lessons learned can be used to avoid the same pitfalls as the prior projects.
- Resources who worked on similar projects can be identified and may be able to help on the new project.
- Leveraging deliverables such as a project charter or project plan can be used as a starting point for the new project, instead of starting with a blank template.

When joining a new project, a project manager should canvass the organization to see similar types of projects (past and current) and understand if they have information that can help with his or her own project.

7. Technique—Align the planning documents. When planning the project, a project manager needs to make sure that all of the documents are aligned. This means that the project plan, resource plan, schedule, cost estimate, and change control log need to be tightly integrated. A common mistake on projects is to create them independently and manage them as separate documents. For example, a project cost estimate may be created based on the number of components, but then not mapped to specific resources or activities in the project plan. There are many results of not having these documents aligned properly:

- Not knowing how the project is progressing against commitments. If the budget and schedule are separate from the plan, it is hard to compare the progress of activities to the forecasted cost and schedule to determine if project goals will be accomplished.
- Not understanding the cost of deliverables. For purposes of estimation or business prioritization, it is helpful to be able to identify the cost of specific deliverables, which requires having the estimates and project plan integrated.
- Not optimal usage of resources. If the resource plan doesn't align closely with the project plan, then resources may be brought on before the work is needed, or they are needed longer than planned for.

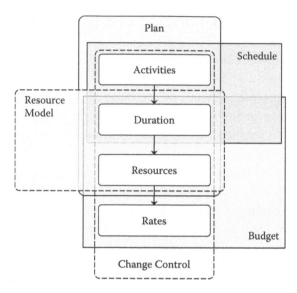

FIGURE 3.3
Alignment of project planning documents.

- Not having clear visibility on the impacts of changes on the project commitments. Without mapping activities to schedule, resources, or cost, it is hard to assess the impacts of changes to the project.

Figure 3.3 shows the relationships between the components of the project planning deliverables. The center column of Figure 3.3 shows that all of the planning deliverables are comprised of the same basic elements:

- Activities—All projects are made up of activities that drive toward specific deliverables and value.
- Duration—The activities take time to be performed.
- Resources—Resources perform the activities.
- Rates—The resources have specific rates or costs.

It is the combination of the basic elements that makes up the different project planning deliverables:

- The project plan is a list of activities with their relationships, durations, and assigned resources.
- The project schedule shows the activities laid out in a timeline with their durations and milestones.
- The resource model identifies the resources used in the project and the duration of their tenure.

- The project cost is comprised mainly of resource costs, which is a function of the resources, their duration on the project, and their cost.
- Change control is managed against anything that impacts the project activities, duration, or costs.

Because the planning deliverables are made up of the same elements, they are tightly related to each other and should be managed as such. Some projects use spreadsheets or project management tools to plan for these components and manage them. These deliverables have to be viewed as living documents and not as one-time activities to create. Impacts of changes and requirement evolution need to be constantly managed to understand the impacts to the project goals.

8. Technique—Identify the critical path. The critical path is the sequence of project activities that aggregate to the longest duration of the project. The critical path represents the quickest possible time to deliver the project. A project can have several concurrent streams of work, but any delay of an activity on the critical path will have an impact on the project schedule.

Identifying the critical path during project planning is important for project managers for several reasons:
- It tells the project manager the shortest duration possible for the project given the list of activities. This allows project managers to manage expectations of stakeholders around the duration of the project.
- It helps the project manager to understand the start and finish dates of activities and their impacts on the project duration. This allows the project manager to understand the flexibility in his or her plans. For example, he or she can lengthen activities outside the critical path without having an impact on the overall project schedule.
- It shows project managers which activities can be "crunched" to shorten the project duration. This can include taking scope out or looking for alternatives.

It allows the project manager to perform "what if" analysis for changes to see the impacts on the overall schedule.

There are several considerations for creating a critical path:
- The critical path may change. Because there are many paths and sequences of activities through the project plan, it is possible for the critical path to change. This can happen if activities that are not on the critical path get extended to a point in which there is a new critical path they are now part of.

- It is not a one-time event. Because of the risk that the critical path may change, project managers should perform the assessment on a regular basis.
- Critical path analysis does not just mean schedule. It should also include the resources required to perform those activities. Understanding which resources are on the critical path may change the resource strategy.

To create the critical path a project manager can use the critical path method (CPM). It was developed in the 1950s by the DuPont Corporation at about the same time that General Dynamics and the U.S. Navy were developing the program evaluation and review technique (Newell and Grashina, 2003). CPM constructs a model of the project that shows its longest path. The results are usually in a network diagram that shows all of the activities and then highlights which ones make up the critical path. CPM also involves identifying the earliest finish time and the latest finish time, with the difference being the "slack" that an activity has to extend without impacting the schedule. There are several modeling tools in the marketplace that can help project managers create the critical path.

9. Skill—Be organized. In order to have a thorough plan and manage the many moving parts, a project manager needs to be organized. Given the nature of their work, most project managers are organized to begin with, but the new environment makes this an even more critical skill. When a project manager is organized, there are many benefits to the project team:

- An organized plan that is categorized by phase or deliverable is easy to understand by the team members. Hundred-line project plans with no structure lend themselves to confusion and lack of clarity around accountability and what to do next.
- Organized project managers stay on top of open action items, issues, and risk and bring them to closure quicker.
- An organized project manager is prepared for meetings, which instills confidence in his or her abilities from stakeholders.

Being organized comes naturally to some people, but there are some activities that a project manager can use to increase his or her structure:

- Observe peers who are very organized to understand their techniques. While every person's approach is different, it is good to see what other people are doing to get a sense of what may work.

- Make lists with categories. Writing down activities is essential to staying organized and is a key tenant for most project management deliverables (plan, action item log, issues log, risk log, etc.). Using categories is also a good way to break down lists into manageable portions. For example, issues can be organized into categories such as resources, technology, business requirements, and implementation.
- Use a personal organization method. Daily planners and personal digital assistants (PDAs) are a good way to manage activities, follow up items, and schedule. There are many tools in the marketplace, and a project manager should try a few until he or she finds one he or she is comfortable with.
- Make time for organization. Being organized has to be seen as an investment that requires time. Block off time each day (beginning of the day or end of the day works well) to organize activities, plan for upcoming meetings, look at items requiring follow up, or look ahead at the project plan to see what needs preparation.

Case Study: Project Planning Discipline: From Strategy to Implementation

Contributed by Kevin Savage

A multichannel distribution program was established by a major auto insurance carrier in an effort to deliver any product through any channel at a rational difference in price. Key elements of the program included (1) pursuing a broader approach to the direct channel (selling insurance directly to customers) and (2) distribution of a long-standing, multi-billion-dollar affinity program through the agency channel (using an agent to purchase auto insurance). In order to be successful, multiple product development projects, heavily leveraging IT capabilities, had to be run in parallel to time market delivery of the same product in different channels. Ultimately, this multiyear strategic program was designed to achieve broader market access and accelerate benefits achieved through economies of scale. The key challenge faced by the program team based on this strategic direction was to design and implement a product in less than eighteen months for sale in both the direct and agency distribution channels. Described below are key challenges faced by this program and how they were addressed by following a well-rounded project planning discipline.

PROJECT DESCRIPTION

Before launching headlong into the market with a new product offering, a program director was hired and a program office established to create an overall master delivery plan. As its first order of business, the program office identified the work to be done, the resources required, and the time/cost/scope parameters of the overall effort. From this point, a market test was designed to assess key features of the product design and determine required supporting capabilities (i.e., sales, service, marketing). Ultimately, the market test sought to assess the merits of a multichannel distribution strategy, enabled by a common product. Following the market test, distribution of a direct-sold product began. Six months later, distribution of this same product through the independent agency channel began, enabling independent agents to sell a special affinity program.

BUSINESS CHALLENGES ADDRESSED

Distribution of a common product through both direct and agency channels at a consistent difference in price mitigated challenges with respect to channel conflict and created the opportunity to put marketing investments to work. Getting to launch required the program office to overcome (1) long-held objections by a national affinity partner regarding agency distribution of their affinity-branded product, (2) agent backlash regarding plans to distribute products directly to consumers, and (3) a protracted delay between the time a product in the direct channel was launched and the time the affinity program through the agency channel was available.

KEY OBSTACLES SURMOUNTED

Once the business strategy was set, work required to deliver a common product to the market in the direct and agency channels consumed a substantial amount of effort, given the resources required to develop business cases, structure project plans, and gain support from multiple stakeholders in a condensed time frame. In order to address key obstacles, a program office was established to manage all aspects of the project life cycle, from analysis and design through to market implementation, following a master program plan. Among the key obstacles faced by the program office were:

- Product development—Multiple products that had been designed to be channel specific in the past could not be easily leveraged to enable a channel-agnostic offering. A common product for sale across direct and agency channels had to be created using a shared IT infrastructure.

- Channel conflict—Concerns from independent agents regarding introduction of a direct product had to be addressed to uphold the carrier's reputation in the agency channel. Both agency and consumer feedback had to be collected up front and brought to bear throughout the project to ensure alignment with the voice of the customer.
- Aggressive timeline—To deliver the affinity program in the agency channel quickly after the direct product was launched, the systems enabling a common product could not be built using traditional IT delivery methods.

HOW THE CHALLENGE WAS OVERCOME

The program office evaluated alternatives and determined best practices to overcome channel-specific differences and eliminate channel conflict by following a pragmatic approach to the setup of the program and ultimately product delivery to market.

- First, regarding product design, the team conducted a due diligence phase to examine existing products and determine the "best fit" class plan for a multichannel offering. The team then designed a common product with consistent pricing differences and shared features.
- Second, conflict in the agency channel was addressed by leveraging the same product design for the direct channel to create an offering that enabled distribution of a national affinity product through agents. Channel noise was mitigated when agent feedback was collected early on in the project.
- Third, regarding time constraints, because both the direct and agency products required delivery to market in tight time frames, product manufacturing was overlapped with IT system design via rapid application development methods. This approach enabled workstreams spanning analysis, design, and development phases to be done at the same time—a highly aggressive approach that resulted in successful delivery.
- Finally, the program office enlisted the help of a communications specialist who executed a robust communications plan that delivered consistent messages to internal and external parties throughout the project life cycle.

WHO SUPPORTED THE PROJECT

The program office gained support by following a collaborative process that consisted of internal peer reviews, participation in strategic planning sessions, senior executive involvement in a monthly steering committee, and regular time/cost/scope checkpoints with project sponsors. The market launch itself required the support and coordinated execution of virtually every functional area (150+ employees), as well as the formation of a dedicated, cross-functional team to execute actions that strengthen the carrier's business model.

WHAT SOLUTIONS WERE ACHIEVED

For the channel expansion effort to succeed, the carrier had to have broad market availability, a highly scalable business model, and best-in-class demand creation capabilities. Project components were structured to achieve solutions for product/pricing sophistication (e.g., common product), media expansion (e.g., brand advertising campaign), structural cost-effectiveness (universal product structure), and demand creation (investments in marketing to benefit all channels). Over time, these solutions will enable cost savings through product rationalization as well as help drive top-line growth.

HOW THIS COMPARES TO SIMILAR PROJECTS

While initiatives followed product manufacturing and IT development methods similar to those of other stand-alone projects, a program on this scale to create a new universal product, open up new distribution channels, and build a holistic brand advertising campaign while renovating technology platforms at the same time had not been done before. The fact that multiple initiatives were executed with overlapping phases to deliver direct and agency products within six months of each other is a significant achievement. This was accomplished through the setup of program office that collaborated with IT to create an integrated master delivery plan, identify interdependencies, develop risk mitigation tactics, constructively manage change controls, and aggressively monitor time, cost, scope, and resources.

HOW CUSTOMER INPUT WAS FACTORED INTO THE PROJECT

Before market launch, the program office leveraged industry studies focused on the carrier's marketplace, analyzed consumer shopping preferences, and assessed brand management best practices in multichannel distribution models. In addition, the program office got help to conduct primary research via agent/customer focus groups to inject customer input into product development and design.

HOW THE TEAM MONITORS/MEASURES SUCCESS

After market launch, the program office worked with an internal research team to capture customer input through satisfaction surveys, audits of service performance, and focus groups with agents. Audits in contact centers are overseen by a dedicated service process owner, and satisfaction surveys to gain input from customers who bought insurance via the agency-sold affinity program are under way. Insights from this research will inform ongoing product and process improvements for the benefit of this carrier's auto insurance customers for years to come.

3.2.2 Use a Standard Methodology for Delivery

As described in Section 2.8, delivery methodologies are commonly used in organizations to standardize project delivery. The primary benefit of a methodology is to have consistency in delivering projects across an organization. Methodologies can be very helpful assets for project managers to plan and run their projects because they outline required steps. They also usually provide templates, guidelines for use, and good examples from real projects that can be used as a starting point. Most methodologies also have critical checkpoints, or phase gates, during the life cycle when deliverables get reviewed or are staged to get approval before moving on to the next stage.

3.2.2.1 Techniques and Skills

1. Technique—Understand deliverables and have checklists. A project manager should become very familiar with his or her company's methodology, including the processes, activities, deliverables, and roles. Knowing the standard deliverables, relationships between them, and the associated roles of the project team members will help when creating the plan and running the project. By including the deliverables and key checkpoints in the project plan, a project manager can make sure that he or she accounts for all required documentation and has the appropriate roles lined up when he or she needs them. Also, using examples and templates provided by a methodology allows the project manager to have a starting point for deliverables, which saves time.

   Most times methodologies have checklists of items to consider that are based on the methodology processes and lessons learned from other projects. For example, there may be a small organization of resources that commonly gets overlooked, and by the time they get engaged in the project, they may not be able to meet the project commitments. In that example, the checklist would remind the project manager to involve that organization early or allow enough lead time in the plan for them. Projects and organizations have become so complex that without checklists, it is very hard for a project manager to consider all of the possible components of the project that need to be planned for.

2. Technique—Focus on value-added activities. As a project manager becomes familiar with the standard delivery processes and activities, he or she can then use his or her own experience and, based on

the project needs, determine which ones add the most value. While there are usually mandatory deliverables, most methodologies have a tailoring step to allow projects to customize which activities they determine appropriate for their project. For example, a smaller project with a tight timeline may choose to use a minimal set of deliverables because their risk of delivery is much lower than that for a larger project, which has a lot of integration points. Project managers need to understand how flexible their organization's methodology is and which deliverables are optional and which are mandatory.

There is always a trade-off between process rigor for project time-lines and commitments. However, there is value to having these deliverables because they force decisions to be documented and con-siderations to be made. Project managers need to work with their process organizations to find the right balance for their projects.

3. Technique—Conduct deliverable reviews. Most delivery methodolo-gies recommend conducting reviews of key deliverables at specific points in time on the project. Conducting these reviews is an effec-tive way to ensure the quality of project deliverables. There are two types of deliverable reviews that should be added to the project plan and resourced.

- Peer reviews. Peer reviews involve having a peer of a team mem-ber review the deliverables before completion or signing off. Examples of this include developers performing code reviews of other developers or a business analyst reviewing a peer's require-ment documentation before going for business signoff. It is always helpful to get a fresh perspective on one's work, especially from someone who is familiar with the project. Peer reviews should be informal in nature.
- External reviews. For critical deliverables a project manager might want a review from someone who is external to the project. This usually involves brining in an expert in a specific domain area. Examples of project deliverables that should have external reviews include:
  - Project estimates (project manager)
  - Project management approach (project manager)
  - Requirements strategy (business analyst)
  - Technical design (architect)
  - Testing strategy (quality assurance)

Case Study: Simple but Diligent

Contributed by Kerry Wills

As a consultant, I have worked on projects for many large corporations. Most of them have standard methodologies for delivering technology solutions. The best example that I have experienced was a company that I worked for that had a very mature set of practices for delivery.

The methodology used was not overly complex with many deliverables. In fact, the main delivery process could be viewed on one page, which then had drill-downs into the specific deliverables. There were also many checklists, templates, and examples that I could use on my project. So instead of starting with an empty project plan, I was able to incorporate the checklists of activities to make sure nothing got left out. I was also able to leverage many of the deliverable examples, which already had sections filled out. For example, the project management approach document had good text for the issue management, risk management, and change management sections, so I simply leveraged what existed. This saved me a lot of time in creating these deliverables.

What I liked about this methodology was that it gave me the guidelines for delivering a project in the organization (with examples), but it wasn't cumbersome. It only focused on the value-added deliverables, which made sure that I planned and executed the project correctly. I have seen this evolution in several companies, where the first iteration of a framework is overly complicated with many deliverables and steps. As the organization matures, it begins to realize that it really only needs a handful of key deliverables, and that the rest don't add as much value for the time that they take to create. The methodology then matures into something simpler and more focused, such as the one in this example.

By having a simple set of processes and leveraging the checklists and examples already captured, I felt confident in my ability to include the necessary components and still meet my project commitments.

3.2.3 Use Resources Intelligently

The most important assets that a project manager has are his or her team members. Project managers must recognize that the ideal of the team working for them is no longer appropriate. What is more likely the case is that the project team is doing the work and the project manager should support them by making sure the issues and risks are addressed. Think of the project as a marathon; the project manager's role is to look ahead of the road and make sure the team can keep running, are well hydrated, and are prepared and willing to keep going. His or her job is to motivate and support the team to keep running, as opposed to just yelling from the sides to go faster.

Because of the criticality in managing project resources, there are several techniques that can be used to ensure that resources are appropriately utilized, planned for, and managed.

3.2.3.1 Techniques and Skills

1. Technique—Engage areas early. Today, most companies have centralized and specialized IT areas that support many different projects and initiatives. Examples include:
   - Infrastructure services
   - Usability design
   - Training creation and delivery
   - Technical platform support
   - Database administration
   - Architects
   - Help desk
   - Release management
   - Specialized technology services, such as Web services, data translation, or content management

   Because these areas are involved in many activities and projects, they don't always have the ability to take on more work quickly. Also, these organizations most likely have specific forms and activities that they need projects to account for. For these reasons, involving them as early as possible is beneficial to a project manager. Failing to reach out to a support group early can mean delays in the schedule and most likely additional cost. By reaching out early, the worst that could happen is the organization would tell the project manager when to engage it, which can be added to the project plan.

   As mentioned in the last section, companies that have methodologies usually have checklists of organizations to involve and reach out to early. If a checklist does not exist, a project manager should start his or her own, but reach out to other project managers or look at historical projects to understand who these groups are.

2. Technique—Involve resources in planning. One of the most effective ways to get team members to buy in to the work and commit to the project is to involve them in the planning of the project activities and schedule. This is a very different approach from the old model where the project manager creates the plan and tells the team what it is and commits to it on behalf of the team. Team members do not feel ownership of

the work or commitments if they are given a date that someone else has committed to without involving them. Involving the team in the creation of the plan and estimates also gains credibility with the project team that the project manager listens to them and respects their expertise.

Involving the team in planning doesn't mean that every team member needs to be included. It should be critical team members who will be accountable for pieces of delivery, which can include:

- Business analyst lead—Understands the business and will be able to articulate the scope of the project. Business analyst leads can highlight business areas that need to be considered in the requirements. They should also be able to articulate activities required of the business for the implementation of the project.
- Architect/design lead—Experienced in the technology options that should be considered when designing the technical solution. Can also provide estimates around the solution design work.
- Technical lead—Aware of the technologies used, systems impacted, and specialized resources needed to deliver the solution. All of these need to be estimated for and included in the plan.
- Testing lead—Understands the different tests needed to ensure quality of the solution, which needs to be planned for.
- Infrastructure lead—Has expertise in the technology platforms and foundational technologies needed to support the solution.

It is often the case that a project has been given a delivery date by the business customer before any estimation is completed. It is a project manager's job to perform a realistic estimate of work based on the team's experiences and then validate this delivery date. If the date is not feasible based on the team's estimate, then the project manager should champion that message back to the stakeholders and present other options to the sponsors (take out scope, change the date, add more resources, etc.). This is sometimes a difficult message to give, but it is based on a realistic estimate from the team, so it is better to state this up front than to explain a variance later in the project.

3. Technique—Have the right skill sets. Because of the increased complexity of projects and the technology used on them, having the right skill sets on a project is critical for success. Usually projects require many different team members from different organizations and vendors with very specific skills. A project manager should look to ensure that the demand for the specialized skills can be met and that the people are available when needed.

The project team also needs to have complementary skill sets across technical domains, business domains, and foundational delivery skills. A project manager needs to recognize the skills needed for his or her project and make sure that the team is comprised of people who possess them. For example, a project manager may recognize that he or she is a strong planner and executor but not a strong communicator. In this case, he or she may want to have a good communications person on the project team. Another example is a project that has several business analysts who all have expertise in one particular business segment, but not in another segment that the project is working on. The project manager would need to supplement the team with someone who has that additional background.

While not every project has all the skill sets needed, a project manager should pay close attention to the skills of the team members and the needs of the project. Projects can probably absorb having a few resources that are not perfect fits, but too many gaps in skills can be a big risk for a project.

Oftentimes, projects are thrown together with available resources that might not necessarily have the right skills. In this case, the project manager should consider the following techniques to make sure that he or she has the right balance of resources:

- Obtain new resources. If resources with the right skill sets are available, then the project manager should look to change out resources for a more experienced resource. Typically, resources don't want to perform poorly, but there is an issue with fit of their skills to the needs of the project. Therefore, replacing resources should not be viewed as a bad thing. This option is rarely available for project managers, and it is often the case that they have to make due with the resources they have.
- Look for mentors. If resources with the skills needed cannot be obtained (which is probably more likely not being able to find new ones), then a project manager can look to find mentors for the project team members who can support them through the work and train them on the job.
- Augment the plan and estimate. Most likely the project plan and estimate were based off of resources that have the appropriate skills to complete the job. If those resources cannot be found, then the project manager should revisit the plan and estimate to account for the increase in duration for the resource to gain the

skills, learn from a mentor, or learn on the job (which also means that rework should be planned for). For example, if a project is using Java technology but all of the developers have Oracle backgrounds and will learn as they go, the project manager should assume a much longer duration than if he or she had a team of expert Java programmers (see "rework" section above).

4. Technique—Provide clarity of roles and accountability. Clarity of project roles is one of the most important ways a project manager can increase the productivity of his or her team. Projects where there are overlaps in responsibilities usually end up with duplicate work efforts, missed activities, and other inefficiencies. As described in Section 2.8, most delivery methodologies come with a roles and responsibility list (also called a RACI diagram), which outlines key roles and their specific accountabilities. A kickoff meeting should be conducted with the project team early on, where clear responsibilities are discussed and documented.

On larger projects, the project manager should consider a matrixed team structure that has horizontal and vertical leads. As Figure 3.4 illustrates, this type of model provides specific accountabilities to the leads. The team leads (verticals) are accountable for the delivery of their teams and the work on their plans. The business and technical leads (horizontals) are accountable for the consistency of delivery, standards, and practices across the different teams. Although there are overlaps, this type of model creates a natural friction to get the work done while making sure that it all ties together well.

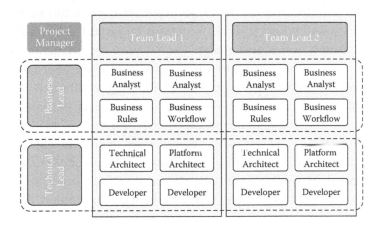

FIGURE 3.4
Project structure with horizontal and vertical leads.

This model is important to use for projects or programs with many work tracks to coordinate the activities. For example, there are two separate teams working on a project. The team leads are individually accountable for the delivery of their components, but there is no one person accountable to coordinate the linkage between the two of them. Therefore, when the project starts to integrate their solutions, they may find that they are not compatible and then have to scramble to redesign the solution or figure out how to make it work.

5. Technique—Leverage experts as much as possible. Referencing the standard guidelines and procedures is important to understanding them, but leveraging experts can yield significant benefits. Oftentimes delivery expertise is spread throughout the organization. Some people have empirical backgrounds in different methodologies such as agile development, rapid application development, or working with vendor partners. Other resources have deep domain expertise in specific technologies or skill sets, such as requirements elicitation.

Project managers should identify and seek out those people in the organization who have the expertise related to their project needs and leverage them (if they cannot get them to work on their team directly). Experts can be used in many ways:

- Estimation of specific components. Experts in a technology or domain understand the intricacies of their areas and can be helpful in creating realistic estimates.
- Consult in the creation of deliverables. Although they may not be able to work on the project directly, experts can be brought in at key points in time to consult on project deliverables. For example, a business analyst can review a requirements strategy from another project to provide guidance on the approach.
- Mentor junior team members. Building additional expertise should be considered when setting up projects so there are not critical resource dependencies on the project.
- Reviews of deliverables. As described earlier in this section, deliverable reviews are an easy way to get high quality with project deliverables. Experts understand pitfalls and complexities and can review deliverables with these things in mind. They also provide a fresh set of eyes to review documents.
- Perform quality reviews. Experts can be used for point-in-time deliverable reviews or phase gate quality reviews.

It is important for a project team to use as much help as possible and not just think they can do it themselves. Chances are that every project can learn something from people outside of the project team and should look to leverage them as much as possible. This will avoid historical pitfalls and produce a higher-quality result.

6. Technique—Determine backup strategy for key resources. Because of the mobile workforce trend, there is always the risk that a critical resource leaves the project or gets pulled onto a higher-priority project. As part of resource planning, the project manager should identify who the key resources are on their project, which can include:

- Resources who are influential to the project, which may include resources who helped define the strategy, resources with special relationships to key stakeholders, or resources who perform a critical function.
- Resources with specialized skills that are in low supply. If these resources were to leave the project, it would have a significant impact on the ability to meet commitments. These are also harder resources to replace.

After identifying the critical resources, a strategy should be documented around how to mitigate or manage the risk of losing that resource. Some techniques can include:

- Having junior resources shadow the more experienced resources to gain their skills and be used as a backup for overflow of work. This has a motivating effect on the person being mentored because it builds their skill sets and shows trust from management.
- Creating succession plans for leads and key members of the teams.
- Creating teams of resources to work together on activities, resulting in having a backup for each resource.
- Recognizing which skills are commodities that can be replaced easily and which skills are harder to acquire.
- Working with management to create incentives for key resources to stay and complete their commitments to the project.

Case Study: Fit for Duty

Contributed by Kerry Wills

I have had many experiences in my career where having the right resources on the team and using them intelligently has been important. I will share some of these examples in this case study.

The first example was on a project that I was managing early in my career. We were a small team made up of a business analyst, architect, business subject matter expert, and the technical team. The business analyst was new to the team, and his resume showed that he had a strong background in facilitating and documenting requirements. When he started working on the project, it was clear that he had a hard time facilitating meetings, gathering specific requirements, and documenting them in a way that the technical team would find useful. He was struggling with the work and was not happy. I was not happy because the quality was poor and we were at risk of missing the project schedule. Since we were a small team, we couldn't absorb any more productivity delays, and we also couldn't absorb the time to bring a new team member up to speed.

Luckily, there was another business analyst on another project team that I was able to leverage to help us finish up the requirements work. At the same time, we had a need for a data analyst to document the data requirements. I decided to give the business analyst resource the opportunity to perform this activity. To be honest, I did not have high hopes for him given the difficulties that he had with the business requirements. To my surprise, he did an outstanding job documenting the data requirements. His mind seemed to work much better around data elements than words and paragraphs.

From that experience I learned that people being successful at their roles is all about their fit for that role. Some people will be more successful in roles that cater to their work styles and thinking than others. It is therefore the project manager's job to make sure that people are aligned to their best fit on the team to maximize productivity and morale.

Another example that I have had in my career was on a program that I was running where there was a project manager who had a very deep technical background. He understood the nuances of the technologies that we were using and could relate to the architects and developers. The problem was that he was not a very good communicator and also did not interact well with the business customers. He would talk to them using technical terms instead of terms that they would understand.

Similar to the first example, I moved this resource into a role that was a much better fit for him. Instead of continuing as project manager, I made him my technical lead, accountable for the technology solution across the entire program. This catered to his background and comfort with technical items and still allowed him to manage a portion of the project. At the same time, it limited his exposure to the business customers and communications. Note that I did spend time coaching him on these areas to build his skills.

In my career, I have had several other examples where having a good fit is important, but the theme is always the same: look for the right fit for people and they will excel at their jobs. No one wants to do a bad job at work, so project managers, as much as possible, should try to align people's work to their strengths and interests. That is not to say that people shouldn't be in stretch roles or work in areas where they can improve their competencies. On projects where timelines are tight and maximizing productivity is important, putting people in the right fit is in the best interest for the person (morale, satisfaction, etc.) and for the project (productivity, better quality, etc.)

3.2.4 Diligent Project Management

Spending the appropriate amount of time up front planning, using a standard methodology, and optimally utilizing resources are great ways to get the project started off well. That same level of diligence should continue throughout the project. Having a good estimate and plan without diligent change control, issue management, risk management, and plan management is not an effective way to ensure delivery of commitments. Projects get reputations of being bad estimators, and a lot of times the original estimate was good, but the execution of the project to those commitments is where the project had challenges and strayed.

Project managers need to stay rigorous and proactive during the entire life cycle of the project. Oftentimes, team members get caught up in the issue of the day or their specific activities. It is the project manager who has to plan ahead and keep the team focused on the goals. This is especially important on projects with long durations because it is easy for team members to think that they have ample time to complete activities.

3.2.4.1 Techniques and Skills

1. Technique—Rigor around the plan and upcoming activities. The new project landscape has many moving parts that the project manager needs to stay on top of. Not managing these activities will lead to the pile phenomenon, where there are piles of work to be done that continue to grow. It is very difficult to manage a project once the piles start to grow because everything becomes reactive to the piles, as opposed to getting in front of the work. Remember that there is no activity on the project plan called "later," and therefore, putting activities off until later is not optimal for success. Some techniques for managing the workload are highlighted below:
   - Understand status of work. Information is critical to understanding where a project is. A project manager needs to ensure that he or she is spending enough time gathering information. This can

be done via status meetings with team members. Another very effective technique is called management by walking around (MBWA), where a project manager blocks off time on his or her calendar to walk the floors (or call off-site resources) to understand where they are on activities. It is important not to fill up the calendar completely, because that impedes the ability to perform MBWA. Information gathered via MBWA is direct since it is on an individual basis and more timely than a weekly status meeting.

- Spend time looking ahead at the plan. Not only should project managers focus on in-flight activities, but they should also spend time looking at the upcoming activities to make sure that they will be ready when the time comes. Several examples of this preparation include:
  - On-boarding resources. If a new resource is planned to join, confirm that it has access to the right systems, paperwork is filled out, what software and hardware are needed, and orientation materials are ready. Reach out to the organization in advance to confirm the commitment.
  - Off-boarding resources. Confirm that the resource will complete its work on time and have the appropriate documentation or knowledge transfer plan.
  - Vendor engagement. Confirm that the procurement and contractual activities are complete. Make sure that any access, hardware, or software needed for the vendors to be productive is set up in time.
  - Technical readiness. Confirm that the appropriate environments, hardware, and software are ready and configured.
  - Meeting preparation. Plan the appropriate materials for stakeholder meetings. Something as trivial as booking a room or a projector could delay a key decision needed to be made.
  - Upcoming deliverables. Confirm that all resources or inputs for the creation of those deliverables will be in place when needed. Follow up on any item that could risk the start of the deliverable.
- Look for opportunities to start work early. If resources are idle (which would be known from walking around), look for opportunities to start other work early.

- Understand the time remaining to complete deliverables. By setting up the project plan at a deliverable level and understanding the effort required to complete the work (called estimate to complete in the earned value framework), a project manager can gauge progress. For example, there is a deliverable that was estimated and planned to be twenty hours. The resource has worked ten hours on that deliverable. Classic project management would say that this means the deliverable is 50% complete. If the resource was then asked how much time it needed to complete the deliverable, the answer may be another twenty hours, which may impact the project cost and schedule. Understanding time to complete is a very good way of measuring progress toward the goals and knowing trends early on.

2. Technique—Constant diligence on operational items. Beyond managing the plan, a project manager needs to spend ample time on the operational aspects of the project. These items are not directly part of the plan but have significant impacts on the outcomes of the project. Each operational item is described below and should be considered an important deliverable for the project:

   - Change control management. The original project estimates are based on an early version of scope. Changes to these assumptions have impacts on the project cost and schedule and have to be managed tightly. Oftentimes projects try to absorb changes only to miss their commitments because of the additional work. There are usually three types of changes that impact a project:

     a. Scope changes. Changes from the original baseline of scope need to be managed using a standard change management process where the change is estimated for impact and approved by the business customer. The cost and schedule forecasts should be updated accordingly. These need to be tracked in a change register to aggregate the impacts, which can then be used to later explain approved variances in the project.

     b. Evolution of scope. When original estimates are made they are completed with high-level scope and many assumptions. As the project goes through the detailed requirements and design phases, its solution becomes more defined. As this happens, the original assumptions may change, which can have an impact on the project cost and schedule. While these aren't necessarily changes in scope, they should be tracked and explained as variances.

    c. Operational changes. As projects progress, there are many operational items that can come up that would impact the project schedule and cost. An example is a project that estimated for resource A at $50 an hour, but that resource left in the middle of the project. Resource A is replaced with resource B, which costs $75 an hour. While the scope did not change, there is a cost impact to switching out resources that needs to be tracked.

- Decision management. Keeping a log of decisions made is an effective way to ensure that there is a history of key decisions. There are many decisions made on projects, and without an audit trail of who made the decision, when the decision was made, and who approved the decision, it is difficult to negotiate conflicts later on in the project.

- Action item management. Beyond the project plan, there are usually action items that come up in team status meetings. These can include conducting a specific meeting, reaching out to stakeholders for follow-up, or acquiring a type of resource. The project manager needs to make sure that the actions get followed up on in a timely manner.

- Issue management. Projects always encounter issues that need to be managed. Escalating them in a timely manner and getting them resolved is a fundamental skill that project managers need to possess. Thinking that project managers can handle it themselves is often a costly mistake. It is always better to provide transparency into the issues so that management can help solve them. Rapid closure on issues is also a very good way for the project manager to gain credibility with the team.

- Risk management. One of the most fundamental, yet least used, techniques in project management is risk management. Projects have tremendous amounts of risks and even more so in the new landscape, with so many stakeholders and moving parts. These risks need to be proactively identified and managed. Oftentimes a risk inventory is taken early on in the project, but it is not a constant process. Project managers should review their risks and gather them from team members at least weekly and put appropriate measures in place to manage them.

- Financial management. Managing the financials of a project needs to be considered a living process. That is, there needs to be a current view of forecasts at all times, including an audit trail

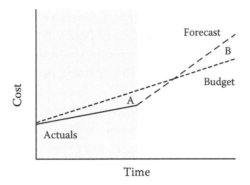

FIGURE 3.5
Estimate at completion.

of changes that can trace back to the original estimates. Project managers should, at a minimum, be tracking estimate at complete (EAC). EAC, as per earned value concepts, is calculated as actual costs to date (ATD) plus estimated cost remaining (ETC). Figure 3.5 highlights an example where the project is midway complete (shown as the double vertical lines) and is currently running a positive variance (A) because its ATD is less than the budget burned to date. However, this is misleading because the project moved some work to a later point and has other unplanned costs that have pushed the forecast (ETC) higher, which will ultimately lead to a negative project variance (B).

- File management. Having an organized structure for project documents is an important way for team members to find key deliverables. Often, organizations that have standard methodologies also have standards for document storage. Absent that, a good technique is to organize the documents in folders that align to the project phases. The number of folders should also be kept to a minimum so information can be found easily. Often, project document sites get cluttered with files and it is hard to tell where anything is. Project managers should consider asking one of the team members to be the project librarian to manage the documents. It is a small amount of effort to keep the library clean, but well worth it for the project team.
- Document management. While most projects try to maintain documentation, it is usually the first thing that gets pushed aside

when projects get into a crunch. However, there are several benefits to having documentation updated:

- The people that will maintain the system after it is released need to understand the history of the system and the detailed requirements.
- An audit trail of decisions and changes is helpful when conflicts arise over the scope of the final product.
- Lessons learned and good examples of deliverables can be used to help other projects.

• Meeting outcome management. Project team members (and especially project managers) spend a large amount of time in meetings. Usually meeting minutes get produced that then get distributed to the meeting participants or team and stored in a file folder. Oftentimes there are decisions made or follow-ups that need to occur. Having a folder of meeting minutes means that team members need to sort through each document to find the relevant information, and it rarely gets revisited. A technique to manage these is to highlight them in the minutes but then track them in a central location. Meeting outcomes should be managed in the action item log, the issues log, the risk log, or the decision log. These can then be communicated, followed up on by the project manager, and reviewed at upcoming meetings. It makes the finding of information easy, instead of trying to remember at which weekly status meeting a specific topic was discussed.

Managing the operational items on a project should be a large part of the project manager's day to ensure that the project is progressing toward its goals and there is transparency into the health of the project. As described in Section 3.2.1, a project manager should consider using a project management office to help coordinate and manage the operational activities.

3. Technique—Establish clear accountability for deliverables and results. To ensure diligence on project activities, a project manager needs to hold team members and leads accountable for specific deliverables and results. This means having clear definitions of responsibilities so team members and leads are aware of what deliverables they are accountable for. Overlapping or unclear accountabilities allow for finger pointing, missed expectations, and confusion on the project.

Some techniques for ensuring accountability on a project include:

- Documenting clear roles and responsibilities so project members are aware of the deliverables that they are accountable for. Beyond having this documented, make sure that it is communicated and understood by team members.
- Each deliverable on the project plan should be owned by one resource. Having multiple names on a deliverable opens it up for people to assume that someone else may be accountable for that deliverable.
- Action items, issues, and risks need primary owners. If these are reviewed at a team lead meeting, then only team leads should have their names assigned. It is difficult to assign someone work and get its status if he or she is not a regular member of the meeting where those items are reviewed.
- Hold people accountable for specific results and not just deliverables. For example, the quality lead should be accountable for the quality of the overall project and not just the testing deliverables.

4. Technique—Make and facilitate quick decisions. One of the biggest challenges on projects is that project managers do not feel that they can make decisions. Part of being diligent and keeping the project moving is to make decisions in a timely manner. Having too many decisions pile up will cause delays and a loss of confidence from the project team.

There are several reasons why a project manager may feel like he or she cannot make project decisions:

- Fear of failure. Project managers may be afraid of making the wrong decision and do not want to have to deal with the consequences of that decision (e.g., management criticism or making things worse).
- Fear of accountability. Project managers may not want to be responsible for the outcomes of the decision if they are wrong.
- Don't feel empowered. Project managers may not think that they have the ability to make decisions.
- Too many options. There may be many options and a project manager is unsure as to which may be the best.

There are several ways that project managers can be decisive on a project:

- Recognize which decisions can be made by them. There are some decisions that a project manager cannot make, such as scope or benefits, but there are many decisions that can be made. These include decisions on resources, sequencing of work, and how to resolve specific issues. For those decisions that project managers cannot make, they should recognize that part of their role is to facilitate those decisions getting made in a quick manner.

- Gather as many facts as possible, but not every fact. It is important that decisions get made using a fact base. That being said, sometimes a decision can be made with enough information, as opposed to spending a very long time to get from 80% confidence to 90% confidence.

- Ask the team for opinions and recommendations. The team is the best set of resources to help make decisions because they are close to the details and understand the nuances of their work. They should be leveraged for input into decisions and to corroborate feedback so that it is not based on one person. Also, getting input from people on decisions is a good way to get support for those decisions and for people to feel empowered.

A project manager should recognize the importance of making quick decisions that are supported by facts and the team's input. Not every decision will be right, but sometimes action is better than inaction. It will be a judgment call for the project manager as to when he or she can make a decision and how best to make it.

Case Study: Taking over a Project Midstream and Instilling Diligence

Contributed by Partha Sastry

The project under discussion was a $4 million two-year initiative by a leading insurance company in United States. The scope was to build a data warehouse solution to consolidate coverage details across all policy writing systems in the company and use this information for analyzing risk exposure to the company.

I took over the project when it was in the build phase and noticed many challenges, including the following:

1. It involved interaction with different application owners across various departments within the company.
2. There was tight coupling with a Web application team being built in parallel with the data warehouse (under the same program).
3. There were multiple groups involved for various activities, including a release management team, a hardware team, a database team, and a sourcing company for development work.

4. The team was disparate and comprised of twenty-five employees, contractors, and resources from an outsourcing company.
5. I had no direct control over the project resources.
6. I also had no direct control over the other departments in the company that were needed.
7. There were not a lot of detailed project management artifacts on the project, which led to confusion and lack of clarity.

PLANNING, TRACKING, AND CONTROL

The most important aspect of project management is to have a workable and detailed plan. This was missing when I took over. The team members were unaware of the tasks and timelines that were expected of them. The responsibilities of the team members were also not documented, and the team had only a vague understanding of their roles and responsibilities. I created a detailed roles and responsibilities matrix to avoid confusion and grey areas.

Many of the meetings were conducted without any reference documents, such as the project plan, issue log, etc. My first priority was to work with the team leads to create the detailed project plan and circulate that with all of the team members. These plans were also walked through in meetings with the team to get their buy-in.

Weekly status meetings were held to check progress. I met with individual teams on a weekly basis and with the entire team every two weeks for status reports. This meeting was also used to discuss any common issues and resolutions.

During the integration testing with the Web project, daily "stand-up" meetings were set up to track status, plan ahead, and discuss issues. These meetings were held in an open area in the office. Even when meetings did not show up on calendars (because the recurrence had stopped and a new meeting invitation had to be sent), team members assembled at the location at a particular time of the day!

ISSUE MANAGEMENT AND DEFECT MANAGEMENT

There were a lot of departments within the company that were providing data to the data warehouse. These teams were not directly reporting to me or even the program manager. Schedule compliance from these groups was absolutely essential to meet the deadlines, so we needed to know quickly any risks to meeting the schedule. We implemented a meticulous issue tracking process. Depending on the number and severity of the issues, meetings were held with the external teams on a daily or weekly basis to resolve issues. For any unresolved issues, the matter was taken to the program manager, who in turn had to use his influence in the organization to get the issues resolved.

Defects were also tracked very meticulously on a daily basis. A daily e-mail was sent to all of the stakeholders on the defects that were assigned to them. The very fact of seeing their name assigned to tasks made the team members act quickly on the issues/defects assigned. This improved the turnaround time of issues and defects.

RELATIONSHIP BUILDING

When I took over, documentation had hardly been done on the project. Every meeting (requirements, design, and status) had ten to fifteen people attending, at the end of which there were no action items and no minutes recorded. I did not have the authority to demand that the senior folks on the team do the documentation. What I did was to take ownership and start documenting the minutes of meetings, action items, design documents, User Acceptance Test (UAT) plans, etc. Over a period of time some of the senior folks realized the importance of documentation and they themselves started documenting.

Over time I became very close with the team members, often spending a lot of time at their desks. Team members normally went out for lunch on Fridays or when someone left the team. I made it a point to attend all those lunches. This helped to build good relationships with team members. These relationships then helped in influencing project decisions. In the end, many of the independent contractors perceived me to be a mentor and often asked for guidance from the PM.

As a result of the diligence that was introduced around the project plan, issue management process, and defect process, we were able to identify issues early for management attention and ultimately meet our project commitments. This was a significant accomplishment given the number of divisions and interaction points that we had to work with, but had no control over.

CONCLUSIONS

Here are some conclusions that can be drawn from the above case study:

1. Create detailed project plans and get team buy-in on timelines.
2. Create a roles and responsibilities matrix.
3. Meticulously track tasks, issues, and defects. Meet with team members regularly (MBWA).
4. The project manager should be willing to get his or her hands dirty by working on some tasks (wherever he or she can add value—design, documentation, test plans etc.)
5. Ensure minutes of meetings are recorded and documentation is done.
6. Build relationships with team members to influence decisions.

3.2.5 Use Metrics Appropriately

The use of project metrics is an effective means to monitor and manage the project and regularly understand its progress and trends. Tracking and reporting on metrics has many benefits to project stakeholders:

- The project manager understands the health of the project and the progress that the team is making toward goals.
- Project team members can understand the goals and how they are progressing toward project commitments.
- Management can gain visibility into challenging areas that may require attention or additional action.

There are several metrics that can be created and tracked to understand different aspects of the project:

- Project schedule variance. The project plan should have a baseline schedule with milestones. A good practice is to have frequent milestones in a project so that the project manager can gauge the progress made toward the project goals. Having milestones every six months is hard to manage because it is not clear until the end of month 5 if the project will meet its goals.
- Project cost variance. As mentioned in the last section, estimate at complete tracking is a good technique to track real-time financial progress against the budget and forecast the final project cost.
- Project scope variance. Because projects today are usually long in nature and have many requirements, it is important to monitor and report on the scope of the project. Meeting schedule and cost commitments but not delivering required functionality can be considered a failed project. Scope can be tracked in number of requirements and needs to be traced through all stages of the project to ensure that the agreed upon scope gets delivered at the end of the project.
- Project quality. Not only does the scope need to be delivered, but it needs to work as intended. The number of defects should be monitored and reported on frequently. The quality of the delivery of a project can be determined by looking at defect rates. For example, projects with high numbers of open severe defects after several cycles of testing are more likely to have quality issues in production than

projects that have closed most of their severe defects and had the chance to retest them in a few cycles.

- Project operations. Metrics can be created to monitor the operations of a project, including the number of open issues, existing risks, change controls, and upcoming demand for project resources.

Some organizations have standard project metrics that they use or standard reports that can be generated from project management tools. In the case where standards don't exist, project managers will need to assess their tool sets to see what metrics are feasible to obtain, track, and report on.

3.2.5.1 Techniques and Skills

1. Technique—Focus on the right metrics and behaviors. The project manager should work with the project sponsor(s) and management team up front and early in the project life cycle to determine which metrics are appropriate and how they can be measured and reported on. Metrics are important but can be misleading, and may push the team in a direction to meet a specific metric, which may not be in line with the project's goals or direction. For example, monitoring the number of completed pieces of code may be the primary metric for progress of development, but if the metrics ignore the number of defects, then they may reinforce a behavior of completing the work quickly without having a focus on quality and testing properly.

   Metrics are useful in that they have the ability to monitor project progress and trends and allow a project manager to see upcoming issues and risks. However, oftentimes project managers or teams are reluctant to identify issues or risks because there is a belief that either they won't come to fruition or they can be resolved without the project sponsors/partners becoming aware of them. This may be the case some of the time, but not the majority of the time. This means that the project manager must have the insight and courage to escalate issues and risks at the earliest indication so that proper decisions and mitigation strategies can be implemented. The project manager's role must move from traditional status taking toward more of a champion and leader whose main job it is to communicate and make issues visible as early as possible. Having a good set of metrics that show the right information is critical to understanding these issues and trends early. The importance of early communication and often will be described in Section 3.4.

2. Technique—Get credible metrics. The project manager needs to understand where the authoritative source of information is for the metrics that he or she wants to report on. Some organizations store project information in several places, and it can sometimes be conflicting or misleading. For example, a project manager may calculate project cost based on time sheets and using a blended rate. The finance organization may use salaries of the team members to calculate the same information. It is always bad when a project manager reports on his or her project in one way and then a different report shows conflicting metrics. This can result in the project manager losing credibility with stakeholders and management.

By identifying and using the authoritative sources of information, confidence in the project metrics can be sustained and metrics can be used for its intended purpose. This allows the conversations to focus on the key messages and not on the confidence or source of the information.

3. Technique—Using metrics for informed decisions. Project managers should have their pulse on the project, and therefore when they raise items for management attention, those items should be fact based. For example, it is not enough to tell management that the project will miss a date without supporting that with the background, cause, remediation, and impact to the project. Having diligence in the operational items and metrics mentioned above should be sufficient for having the right information to use when raising items for attention. This is referred to as "speaking with data" or "speaking with facts" to ensure that the complete picture is being presented.

Sometimes all the facts are not readily available and the project manager must decide if raising an issue early is more important than getting all of the details. By their nature, project managers want to control their projects and believe that they can handle any challenge that arises, but it is important to show transparency to project stakeholders. One way to represent this information is by using the following status categories, which highlight the amount of management attention that is required:

- Risk—Something that may happen to the project and needs to be managed.
- Challenge—Something that is currently happening on the project but isn't causing an impact yet. Management should be aware but no action is needed.
- Issue—Something that is currently happening on the project and is causing an impact. Management action is needed.

Case Study: Managing toward the Wrong Metrics

Contributed by Randy Wills

I was a project manager at an insurance company in Ohio managing a large system conversion effort using an agile software development approach. The project was a multiyear system conversion to consolidate all of our websites into a single technology for agents, insureds, and call center resources.

I was managing three concurrent teams. Each team would handle a single piece of functionality, such as adding a vehicle, changing an address, adding a driver, billing, etc. Even though the teams had independent pieces of functionality, they had to work together to coordinate programming, testing, and defects since all three teams were working in the same technical environment. This required a lot of coordination to ensure that there were synergy and good teamwork.

Since the project was extremely visible at the highest corporate levels due to cost, impacts, and benefits promised, early on during the project start-up I was asked to provide a weekly metric dashboard that was easy to understand. My dashboard consisted of different project metrics, including key project dates, progress toward those dates, number of defects per functionality, key risks, and key issues.

To help make the team aware of these metrics, I would post them around the team's workspace and send them out via e-mail so that everyone knew what was being measured and where the team was against those metrics. In the agile methodology, this is referred to as information radiators, which reinforces everyone's understanding of what metrics are being monitored. This worked out well in ensuring that the team knew the importance of the metrics being monitored.

The three concurrent teams had a lot of interdependencies since they were working in the same technical environment, where one team could easily inadvertently disturb another team's programming with defects or breaking the technical environment. Teamwork, communication, and coordination were essential to the success of this project. There were a total of twenty developers on the three work teams that had to work together and be aware of the technical changes that they were working on.

To help manage the performance of the twenty individual programmers toward the greater team's goals, I tracked metrics on each of the resources, such as scope delivered (i.e., amount of work programmed) and number of defects per scope item (i.e., quality of work). During each one-on-one I would discuss with the programmer how much work he or she had achieved over the two weeks since the last discussion and the quality of the work. While this seemed like an excellent way to manage individuals to determine performance, what it was actually doing was taking away from the ability to function as a team.

Initially, the teams worked very well together. There was frequent communication, developers helping other developers when questions came up, sharing of ideas and best practices, and the team was thriving. As I began having one-on-ones with the developers and continued having discussions on productivity, the morale of the team began to change. The developers quickly realized that their performance was being evaluated against each other's based on the amount of work produced and number of defects. This started leading to developers not wanting to share best practices since in essence they were helping their peer's individual metrics improve, while taking time away from their own productivity. By helping their peers resolve defects and answer questions, they were also helping to make their peer's quality look better. Over the next few weeks, the team's morale had decreased, and as a result, the team as a whole was producing less quality programming.

As it became apparent that the team's productivity and morale was decreasing with each passing week, I realized what was at fault and immediately stopped producing and discussing individual metrics with the team members. I also called a team meeting to announce that the individual metrics were being stopped and that the team metrics were what the team would be graded on.

I learned a valuable lesson: metrics are important, but they can sometimes take the focus away from the intended goals of the project team as a whole. People tend to focus on what they are being measured on, and this case study shows how mismanaging metrics can lead to morale, quality, and team cohesiveness issues.

3.2.6 Improve Competencies

To maximize the effectiveness of project rigor, a project manager should focus on building his or her core competencies of project delivery. Having an empirical background in the key areas of the project has many benefits:

- Demonstrate credibility—Team members value and respect leaders who understand their areas of work. This increases the project manager's ability to be influential on the project resources.
- Talk the same talk—Having a background in different aspects of the project allows the project manager to understand what the team members are saying and speak in their same language.
- Understand the context—Because the project manager understands the context for the project, he or she can see how the different pieces of the project tie together. This makes the project manager much more effective at driving direction, understanding implications, and facilitating sessions to desired outcomes.

- Communicate to different audiences—Grasping the different aspects of a project allows the project manager to change his or her communication style and messaging based on the particular audience. Translating technical messages to business people, or business goals to technical people is an important technique to make sure the team is working toward the same goals.
- Facilitate and make better decisions—Because roles are becoming more specialized and focused, projects today rarely have people who can see across the different aspects of a project. By understanding the relationship of project roles, a project manager can better understand implications when planning or managing a change. Also, having a broad understanding of the business or technologies being used on a project allows the project manager to help facilitate decisions between different stakeholders by appealing to their backgrounds and focus areas.

There are four major areas of competencies required to be a successful project manager in the new landscape, as shown in Figure 3.6.

1. Project management fundamentals. First and foremost, a project manager needs to have the fundamental skills required to execute a project. These skills allow the project manager to manage the different aspects of the project. These skills include:
   - Project planning
   - Project estimating
   - Financial management
   - Resource management
   - Risk management
   - Issue management
   - Scope and change management
   - Communication management
   - Vendor management

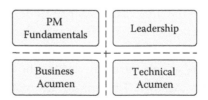

FIGURE 3.6
Focus areas of PM competence.

In addition to project management fundamentals, a project manager should have a deep understanding of the software development life cycle. If possible, this should go beyond just understanding the deliverables, and focus on the relationships between them. Because roles have become so specialized, there is usually a lack of clarity into what each role does and how they interact.

Project managers who have played roles as a business analyst, architect, or tester empirically understand those roles and their relationships to other aspects of the project. This makes them able to plan more effectively for the different components of a project, ensure the appropriate interaction points happen, and even assess the validity of the deliverables. They can also understand the impacts of changes and conflicts as they arise, which allows for a faster resolution.

2. Leadership. To complement the project management fundamental (hard) skills, a project manager also needs leadership (soft) skills. Project management fundamentals allow a project manager to know how to deliver projects and the relationships of the roles and deliverables. However, it is often the softer skills that enable a project manager to be successful in delivering on project commitments. That is because projects are made of people performing the work, and those people need to be inspired and motivated to work toward commitments. These leadership skills will be described in detail in Sections 3.3 to 3.5 and include:
   - Building and fostering relationships
   - Effective communication
   - Facilitation
   - Negotiation
   - Motivating and inspiring the team
   - Empowerment
   - Self-management
   - Being a champion for the team

3. Technical acumen. Beyond having the core skills in project management and delivery methodology, the PM should also have acumen in the technologies being developed on the project. This includes both the applications being impacted by the project and the specific technologies being used to develop the solution.

   Knowing the technologies and systems allows the project manager to have an understanding of the solution being built for the project so he or she can interact more effectively with the technical team. This can include a better understanding of issues, facilitation of decisions, analyzing impacts of changes, and articulating items for management attention. A project manager who can translate a technical challenge into terms that stakeholders and sponsors can understand will be much more successful at getting to closure on issues, as opposed to spending time explaining the problem.

4. Business acumen. Lastly, a project manager needs to have an understanding of the business that his or her project is supporting. This includes the business products, key organizations, distribution channels, and an understanding of how the business makes money. Knowing these will allow a project manager to articulate the vision and benefits of the project to the team. It also allows him or her to interact better with the business customers, sponsors, and subject matter expects. Similar to having good technical acumen, the results will be better project decisions and communications with stakeholders.

There is a belief that generic project management skills are transferable across businesses, technologies, and industries. Project managers don't need to become experts in the technologies or business because there are other roles on the project that focus on these areas (e.g., architect, technical lead, and business analyst). However, they should have enough of a background to be able to have a conversation with those resources in their own language and be able to understand the important elements.

3.2.6.1 Techniques and Skills

1. Technique—Get experience. The best way to build any of the four competency areas is to gain firsthand experience. While there is a belief that project management skills are transferable, it is helpful to learn the business and technical aspects of the organization as well.

    There are a few ways that a project manager can gain these experiences:
    - As project managers progress in their careers, they should be looking for opportunities to grow their project management skills and to serve in the different roles on a project (such as a business analyst, architect, or tester). This experience will round out their understanding of project roles and their relationships to each other.
    - Shadowing resources by following them around is an effective way to see the systems that people use, understand the business processes, and observe the type of work that different roles perform.

- Ask people about their roles—the work that they do, the systems that they work with, and the business that they support. Not only does this provide insight for the project manager, but it also shows interest in people's work (see Section 3.5).
- Look for relevant training. There may be existing training on the business practices, leadership skills, or project management skills that a project manager can attend to improve his or her competencies.

2. Technique—Supplement projects with people to fill competency gaps. In the case where a project manager is thrown into a new situation where he or she cannot ramp up quickly, he or she should look to supplement the project with the appropriate resources. This begins with recognition of where there are competency gaps. For example, a project manager who has a solid background in PM fundamentals and methodology may be new to a business unit and would thus look to have a strong business analyst team with that background. This is not to say that the project manager should not use the techniques listed above to build those competencies, but rather that he should utilize this as a short-term strategy to fill the gap.

Project managers should consider taking an inventory of the people on their team to understand what resources have what strengths and where there might be gaps that need to be filled.

Case Study: Building a Balanced Team

Contributed by Kerry Wills

I was asked to take over a program when it was already under way. This program consisted of several integrations of data warehouses and data marts. I recognized early on that my entire background in project delivery was based on application development and not data integration.

I spent the first few weeks on the program understanding who the key resources were on the team and what their skills were, to make sure that we had the right balance of skills. The analysis of the program resources that I came up yielded the following observations:

- Project manager 1—Long background in project management and some in data warehousing. He was new to the company.
- Project manager 2—Strong background in data warehousing with moderate experience at the company and with project management.
- Lead business analyst—Very experienced at the company and with data warehousing.

- Technical leads—Very experienced with the technologies used and the company, but not much experience in project management.

As a result of the makeup of the resources on the program, I organized it in the following manner:

- Put project manager 1 on the project with the least data integration and aligned him with the business analyst, who could support him in understanding the company's background and business.
- Had project manager 2 manage the heavy data integration project to leverage his strengths in this space. I stayed on top of his plan to make sure that he was supported in the project management activities.
- Had the lead business analyst work across all the projects to provide continuity of requirements, and utilized his experience to the fullest. I met with that person on a weekly basis to get updates and his perspectives on the project work.
- Had the technical leads stay on their separate projects, but introduced a technical project manager who could work across the projects to plan for and manage the technical components. This allowed the technical leads to focus on the technical aspects of the program and not on the project management aspects.

This model proved to be effective because it utilized the strengths of all of the resources, balanced the skills across the program, and filled the gaps that existed. It also allowed me to utilize my strengths while empowering the other team members to own pieces that I was not strong in (such as the business requirements or technical data integration pieces). Therefore, instead of me spending the time getting up to speed on data integration techniques, I could focus on running the program. I did spend some time to understand these areas as the program progressed, but it was not on the critical path to get up to speed first.

I believe that if the skills of the team members were different on this project, then I probably would have made different moves as to how the program was structured. I believe that team structures should be situational based on the skills of the resources on the team, and it is up to the project manager to find the right balance between them to optimize the interaction model for the project.

3.3 CONSULTATIVE APPROACH

Section 3.2 described several techniques for thoroughly managing the planning and execution of a project. These techniques are fundamentally needed to run the mechanics of a project, such as the project plan, issue log, risk log, schedule, resource plan, etc. However, it is the softer skills that are needed to manage the people aspects of the project. Because projects are comprised of teams of people doing the work, having the ability to influence them to meet project goals is much harder, and in many ways more important, than managing the deliverables. The project manager that can work with people and inspire them will be much more successful than a project manager who knows everything that there is to know about risk management but who cannot relate to other people.

As noted in Chapter 2, there are many challenges in managing people on projects due to the changing business landscape and makeup of projects. Some of these challenges include:

- Resources do not report to the project manager. Almost every company today works in a matrixed environment. This means that project teams are comprised of people from many different organizations who have different managers outside of the project work. Project managers need to be able to motivate and influence these resources that they do not have direct control over.

- Resources are fractionalized and have other priorities. Because of aggressive corporate agendas and increased workloads, it is rare that a project gets fully dedicated people. Therefore, critical team members sometimes have competing priorities from other projects that they are working on. The project manager who can distinguish himself of herself from the other project managers asking that same resource for work will be more successful in meeting his or her objectives.

- Project resources may work for different companies. Because of outsourcing, third-party technology products, and specialized skill needs, project teams are usually comprised of both employees and nonemployees (contractors and vendors). Project managers need to take a different approach to manage the vendor resources than they do to manage company employees.

- Resources are specialized. As projects get bigger and technologies become more complex, there is increased resource specialization. This results in having people working on very finite portions of the project, and as a result, they don't always see the bigger picture they are working toward. The project manager must provide this vision and cohesion to the work.

- Resources are mobile and fickle. If team members are not challenged properly or not motivated for any reason, they may look for different opportunities elsewhere. Because of some of the trends in business, the days of employees staying at one company for thirty years are gone.

TABLE 3.2

Categories of Power

Category	Description
Legitimate power	Power of an individual because of the relative position and duties of the holder of the position within an organization. Legitimate power is formal authority delegated to the holder of the position.
Referent power	The ability to influence others based on interpersonal relationships and the ability to build loyalty. It is based on the charisma and interpersonal skills of the power holder. A person may be admired because of a specific personal trait, and this admiration creates the opportunity for interpersonal influence. Here the person under power desires to identify with the personal qualities of the leader, and gains satisfaction from being an accepted follower.
Expert power	The ability to influence others based on one's skills, knowledge, experience, or expertise. It is a function of the amount of knowledge a person has relative to the rest of the team members in the group or project.
Reward power	The ability to influence others based on control over desired resources, such as money, gifts, or promotions.
Coercive power	The ability to influence others through the application of negative influence or the removal of positive events. It might refer to the ability to demote or withhold other rewards. It's the desire for valued rewards or the fear of having them withheld that ensures the obedience of those under power.

As a result of the evolution of resource engagement on project teams, the project management leadership style also needs to evolve. In their classic study on the bases of power, social psychologists John R. P. French and Betram Raven identified five categories of power (French and Raven, 1959), described in Table 3.2.

In the old business landscape, project managers had authority over project resources and mostly focused on using legitimate, reward, and coercive power. Today, since most resources are not direct reports, these techniques are less effective. Also, because of the complexities of technologies and business process on projects, it is hard for a project manager to have expert power in the technologies or business.

In the current environment the project manager must rely mostly on referent power, and therefore must take more of a consultative approach toward resource management and his or her interaction with project

TABLE 3.3

Possible Impacts of Resource Management Styles

Resource Type	Authoritative Style and Result	Consultative Style and Result
Matrixed resources	Direct and controlling style does not work when resources don't report to the PM and will result in resentment, poor morale, lack of information sharing, and poor quality.	Influencing and motivating will result in understanding status, being made aware of issues earlier, and achieving goals with a motivated team.
Fractionalized resources	Commanding resources who are part-time on a project will result in a lack of responsiveness and focusing on work for other project managers (who treat them better).	Negotiating and influencing skills will result in a higher prioritization of work and more attention to project needs.
Nonemployees	Aggressive management of nonemployees will result in them not "going the extra mile" for the project, and possibly leaving for other opportunities (contractors are typically very mobile).	Influencing and soft skills will result in motivated members who will want to continue to produce high-quality work on a project.
Specialized resources	Directing specialized resources will get the work done but may not integrate well into the bigger picture.	Facilitating and gathering information will result in tighter coordination between components of the project.

stakeholders. Having an authoritative style of management in this current environment can be detrimental to the project. Table 3.3 demonstrates some examples of using an authoritative style vs. a consultative style for managing project resources and what those impacts might be.

There are several techniques and skills that a project manager can use to become more consultative in his or her approach toward interacting with the resources and stakeholders on the project. As shown in Figure 3.7, the project manager must focus on his or her ability to influence others, build relationships, and understand the political landscape of the company, and how to navigate it successfully. Beyond the external activities, project managers must also be able to manage themselves in any project situation.

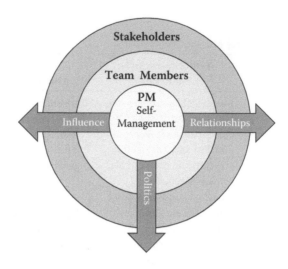

FIGURE 3.7
Consultative approach dimensions.

3.3.1 Relationship Focus

At the heart of the consultative approach and using referent power is a focus on building and leveraging relationships. This includes relationships with the many different people involved with the project:

- Team members, to understand status, identify issues and risks as early as possible, and help to solve problems
- Resource managers, to acquire project resources at the appropriate time with the appropriate skills needed
- Managers and sponsors, to communicate, escalate, and get decisions from
- Customers, to solicit feedback on the project and its requirements
- Vendor partners and contractors, to plan and manage activities

There are several techniques to focusing on successful relationship management, but they need to be considered as an investment in time and intentionally planned for and performed. A project manager must treat relationship management as being as important as project planning or financial management.

3.3.1.1 Techniques and Skills

1. Technique—Involve people early. As described in Section 3.2.3, the project manager should involve key team members in the planning

of the work. Not only does this help with increasing the accuracy of planning and gaining commitment to the goals, but it also strengthens the relationship between the project manager and the team. Involving team members in the planning shows a trust between the project manager and those team members. This trust is critical to build early in the project so that when the project hits roadblocks the team can work together to overcome them.

Sometimes project teams have "difficult" team members who have worked in the company for a long time and don't necessarily care for planning, project management, or communications (and tell everyone who will listen about it). It is especially important to involve these people in the planning and get their buy-in. It is very hard for them to be vocal against a plan that they helped to create.

2. Skill—Build relationships before issues. Building relationships early during a project is critical to success for project managers. It is important to have established a relationship early on a project so that when the contact is called upon when something is needed, it is not the first time that there is an interaction with this contact. This way it is more of a friend calling in a favor, as opposed to being seen as just calling because he or she wants something.

The project manager should start with understanding and identifying who the influential people for the project are. That might include key team members, resource managers, vendor partners, or sponsors. Then the project manager should set up a strategy to build a relationship with those people, which can include the following techniques:

- Setting up an initial conversation to discuss the project. In the first meeting, discuss the project, background, scope, and expectations of the roles. Recommend to schedule follow-up meetings, and as they become more frequent, look for opportunities to build a deeper relationship.
- Looking for things in common with that person. One effective method is to schedule an introductory meeting with that person in his or her office. Once in the meeting the project manager can glance around the office to look for something that he or she might have in common with that person. This can include having children, photographs from places they have both been to, having a college, sports teams, or hobbies such as fishing or

hiking in common. Be sensitive to bringing up personal information early in a relationship, though, as this technique could backfire if the person is not comfortable sharing his or her personal activities after just meeting someone. If the conversation is more social, then this technique can work, but if the conversation is purely business, then follow the person's lead and let the relationship evolve.

- Set up regular meetings to catch up. If the contact is a peer, based on the situation, the project manager may want to use an informal setting such as a coffee shop or cafeteria to foster the relationship.
- If the person is in the same building or company complex as the project manager, the project manager should consider stopping by occasionally to say hello and catch up on project or nonproject topics.
- Look for opportunities to do small favors for people. While there shouldn't be a feeling of being owed something in return, it does set the stage for future negotiations. This can include helping with a presentation, sharing a skill such as creating spreadsheets, or letting the person borrow a resource if a crisis comes up.

Depending on the company culture, some of the above-mentioned techniques may be more or less effective. Some company cultures are very formal and professional, which would cater to meetings on specific topics and sticking to that agenda. Other companies may be more social and network based. The project manager should understand the cultural environment of the company before creating the relationship strategy.

By building relationships with key people early and fostering them as the project progresses, it is easier to leverage those relationships as issues or conflicts arise. This can also be very effective for working with shared service team members who have competing priorities from other projects. It is human nature to help out acquaintances more than people who aren't known as well. When a shared service resource has requests from four or five project managers to perform work at the same time, having an established relationship may make a project manager first on that person's list.

Building successful relationships is a combination of the above-mentioned techniques and practice. A project manager should consider the following activities to build his or her skills around successful relationship management:

- Observe other successful project managers to see how they approach project relationships. Make note of what works and what doesn't based on the approach and the people involved.
- Understand the corporate culture to see what is acceptable and not acceptable regarding professional relationships.
- Gain experience for what works and feels natural to the project manager. If a project manager is uncomfortable with fostering relationships, then the approach may come across as fake or awkward. It is imperative that the project manager come across as genuine in his or her interactions with people.

Case Study: Relationships That Focus and Influence Outcomes in a Social Responsibility Project

Contributed by Carin Salonia

I was a program manager at a large insurance company in the Northeast United States managing a thirty-thousand-employee United Way Campaign effort. Managing the campaign effort is highly regarded and considered a leadership development opportunity in the company. The effort engages emerging leaders identified by senior executives in corporate, home, and field offices. We have an enterprise opportunity to promote awareness, participation, and increase community involvement and donations during the annual United Way Campaign. The United Way is a nonprofit organization that is focused on working with partner agencies, volunteers, and community leaders in initiatives that change conditions to improve lives in the community it serves. My role in this effort was to function as the enterprise chairperson, leading the steering team to develop strategies, implement the plan, and deliver the results for the campaign. Our steering team consisted of an executive sponsor, four co-chairs, two marketing and communications team leads, the leadership giving chair, one data analyst, and sixty office ambassadors. Our team completed an on-boarding process that included dialogue and training with key leaders from the United Way, as well as past campaign leaders, and lessons learned documentation. Our campaign was prescheduled and lasted three weeks.

The annual United Way Campaign provides an opportunity for corporations to support nonprofit organizations aligned with their communities and demonstrate a commitment to a community relationship. Alignment to the communities in which the organizations are located provides a unique opportunity for corporate giving and visible community involvement by the organization and its employees. Making connections through the visible partnership of an organization with its community can have a powerful impact on both employee morale (a reason to be proud of the company) and employee loyalty (employee recruitment and retention), as well as impact the financial results of the company and the campaign (relationship of myself or my company to others in "doing good" and agencies supporting local businesses).

Developing effective relationships cannot be understated in any project, but it is especially important in a social responsibility project. In this type of project, most of the team members are volunteers or recruits. The team members may be involved because they have a personal connection and can identify with the effort, or have been asked to add it to their list of other priorities, or both. Given the matrixed and dispersed team composition for the United Way Campaign, our team met several weeks prior to the campaign's launch to define our goals and develop our strategies, outreach, and communication plan for the three-week campaign period. During the campaign we conducted two meetings per week focused on results and strategies to improve or meet target goals. Some of the mid-campaign activities included key messages from leaders to divisional staff, events that highlighted awareness and participation (coffee or lunchtime meetings, casual dress-down day), and leadership rallies to support communication around our goals.

Some of the challenges that we faced included a dramatic change in the economic climate over the prior year. Several reductions in workforce across the major corporations supporting United Way and internal reductions within the organization had occurred. A downturn in the economy and the impact on our organization resulted in some emotional disengagement, a lingering fear of layoffs, and a loss of trust as we planned our campaign. State and local calls for food, services, and assistance had increased by 80% over the prior year. Our challenge was to develop a comprehensive "call to action" campaign that engaged executive leaders, leadership givers, and employees in both home and field offices to give of their time and financial resources in a difficult and uncertain economic time for many. Our challenge was to focus community commitment and leverage the core values of our organization and link to doing good for others. Our challenge was to feel good again as an organization, as a community of networked professionals whose core values are about helping people.

Core to our strategy was leveraging existing relationships across the organization and developing new ones external to the organization. Our strategies for leveraging relationships across the organization included:

1. Continuation of a previously successful ambassador program to align committee campaign staff to existing business units with like services or locations (peer-to-peer engagement). This allowed people to connect to the ambassadors because they were from the same organizations vs. someone from outside the organization.
2. Development of a leadership giving committee to engage leaders with leaders, communicate leadership level giving and philanthropic

responsibilities, and develop goals for leader performance across the organization.

3. Promote connections through personal stories of the company's employees that have utilized agencies supported by the United Way. This allowed people to internalize and relate to the key message of the campaign.

4. Highlight leadership thoughts and involvement in the United Way and personalize why giving to the United Way is important to "me," personally and professionally. Demonstrate visible leadership engagement with messages on core values of the company and commitment to the community.

Some of the strategies for leveraging relationships external to our organization included:

1. Engage relationships with community agencies by sharing stories of the need for community support and services, and promote connections of "We all have something to give."

2. Leverage affinity groups/social networks currently in place in the corporation and engage United Way in a focused manner for these social mediums.

3. Have weekly engagement calls with the United Way liaison, developing a relationship of understanding, influence, and inclusion in activities.

During this time frame we identified and solicited senior leaders for their visible participation in audio and e-mail messaging, developed personal stories, and engaged in several events. We delegated engagement of senior leaders through prior relationships—those on the steering committee who had previous working relationships could leverage those relationships for engagement for the campaign.

Developing goals, strategies, and monitoring the progress of our campaign required a top-down engagement of our executive leaders and bottom-up and wide engagement of our dispersed employee base. We developed a detailed communication plan that promotes emotional connections and relationships among our organization leaders, staff, and community. Daily results of the campaign metrics (response rate and donation rate) were shared with the steering committee, ambassadors, and senior leaders. Business units monitor their progress and cascade messages of performance against the goals of participation/response rate and overall dollars raised. This promoted continued interest and engagement. Overcommunication is possible (considered nagging), so focused e-mails from specific leaders to their constituents were scheduled to reduce overlap or multiple messages being sent.

We had an amazing campaign year—a highly visible campaign that exceeded the multi-million-dollar goal by 18%, an increase in response rate by 11%, and a 100% increase in volunteers participating in the Day of Caring. Anecdotally, many employees who engaged in the campaign this year felt proud, connected, and more committed to a community-minded relationship.

In this project, it was important to identify and leverage both internal and external relationships to meet the common goal, inspiring those through doing good and developing new understandings and relationships. We all want to feel connected, important, and part of something bigger. This was a great project experience that demonstrated the importance and power of relationships and the impact those relationships can have in influencing and achieving our goals.

3.3.2 Influencing

Focusing on relationships is critical to building bonds between the project manager and the resources needed to complete the project. Just knowing people, however, is not enough to get them to do the activities necessary to complete the project. This is where the skill of influencing becomes crucial for the project manager to have. It is especially important in the current environment for the following reasons:

- Resources do not report to the project manager, and therefore there is no formal authority for the project manager to use to get resources to perform the work.
- Resources are tasked with many activities that often compete for time with the needs of the project manager. Being able to influence those resources or their management to meet project commitments is necessary at times for the project.
- There are many stakeholders on the project who have different opinions as to the vision, scope, and direction of the project. These need to be reconciled for a project to avoid "spinning" in cycles during it.
- On a daily basis, decisions need to be made on a project that involve working with other stakeholders. These decisions usually require presenting background on the decisions with some recommendations. A project manager needs to be able to influence others to make the decisions that best impact the project goals.
- Conflicts and issues arise on the project and need to be dealt with quickly but thoughtfully so that all parties feel there are successful outcomes.

Each project manager has a different style and approach to influencing others because it has to be natural behavior or it doesn't come across as genuine (and therefore doesn't work). For example, some project managers use humor and approachability to influence people. Others may use deep acumen in business or a strong professional network. The company culture also has an impact on what styles are more effective than others. Some companies may use data and metrics to influence decisions, whereas others may be more focused on interpersonal communication and relationships.

Most of the recommendations in the book so far have focused on specific techniques needed to be a successful project manager. Influencing is more of a set of personal skills than specific techniques, and therefore the next section will describe these skills, highlight considerations when using them, and suggest ways of continuing to strengthen them. A project manager should think about using several different methods to influence others and modify his or her approach based on the corporate culture, the individuals involved, and the results he or she is achieving from those methods.

3.3.2.1 Techniques and Skills

1. Skill—Persuasion. Persuasion is the ability to convince another person to do something. There are many instances on a project where a project manager will need to persuade stakeholders. Some examples include:
   - Asking project team members to do work and meet project commitments without having direct authority over them. This is especially difficult for resources that are fractionalized and also working on other projects.
   - Asking managers and stakeholders for resources or information that is needed on the project.
   - When setting expectations with stakeholders, persuading them with the reasoning behind his or her information.
   - Raising issues or risks to project sponsors and getting buy-in and approval for the recommendations.

   According to Aristotle, rhetoric is "the ability, in each particular case, to see the available means of persuasion." He described three main forms of persuasion: ethos, pathos, and logos. Each of these can be used depending on the situation.
   - Ethos is appeal based on the character of the speaker. An ethos-driven document relies on the reputation of the author. This is where the personal credibility of the project manager plays a role.

Sometimes it is helpful to start a conversation to establish this credibility. For example, if there is a technical issue that needs a decision, a project manager may bring in some of the technical experts on the team and introduce them as such.

- Pathos is appeal based on emotion. This is where a person is persuaded based on his or her set of values. This may be a way to motivate the team toward meeting project goals or rallying them around a crisis.
- Logos is appeal based on logic or reason. This means persuading people with facts and information. This is especially effective when asking management for a decision or in a crisis where action is needed.

There are several things to keep in mind around persuasion:

- Try not to appear to be going to great lengths to persuade somebody. It must come across as genuine and not as manipulative (ethos).
- Don't preach too much or people will just close their options to the point where influence has been lost on them (ethos).
- Try to relate to the audiences (ethos).
- Show people the benefits of the idea, specifically geared toward how it will impact them (pathos).
- Prepare for any contradictions by considering the audience and what push back might be given (logos).

2. Skill—Presence. Building on persuasion skills, a project manager also needs to have presence. This means that a project manager projects a sense of self-assurance and confidence in his or her leadership skills. This is an essential skill to influencing others because it demonstrates confidence and conviction, which are needed to successfully facilitate, negotiate, present recommendations, and persuade others.

There are several ways that a project manager can focus on improving his or her presence:

- Dress the part. Project managers should always dress in a professional manner, which shows respect for their work, themselves, and their team. Project managers should consider dressing fancier (e.g., business suit) for meetings with senior executives or customers. However, project managers should consider the organizational culture and team culture when they dress. Sometimes wearing a business suit every day can come across as pretentious or being "above the team members." Conversely, the project manager may not want to dress down often and be seen as too casual and not get the team's respect.

- Talk the part. Project managers should be conscious of the words they are using and how they speak. It is very hard to influence others, negotiate a crisis, or facilitate a heated discussion when speaking softly and quietly. Conversely, coming across as too loud can be seen as dominating and authoritative. A project manager should be confident in his or her speech and use intonation to highlight key points in his or her messages.
- Act the part. Project managers should recognize that they are leaders and that they are constantly being watched by the team members. Therefore, if project managers act like the leader of their team, they will be perceived that way. However, if they act like they don't have control over the project and cannot make decisions, then they will quickly lose the confidence of the team.

Project managers should not confuse having presence with being arrogant or self-promoting. Being self-assured is very different from stating one's experience and importance to others. There is a fine line between confidence and arrogance, and the project manager should use the self-management techniques identified in Section 3.3.3 to get an understanding of how he or she is perceived.

3. Skill—Successful facilitation. Facilitation is the art of coordinating people to produce a common goal, such a making a decision on the requirements or design of a solution, resolving a project issue, or simply sharing information. This usually happens in the context of a project meeting where the project manager plays the role of the facilitator. This requires the following activities:

- Preparing for the meeting by setting an agenda, inviting relevant stakeholders, and sending out any prereads in advance of the meeting
- Running the meeting and ensuring that agenda topics get covered, the team stays focused on the meeting goals, and ideas get brought up in a safe environment
- Documenting meeting results, key decisions made, and next steps
- Following up on action items

At the core of successful facilitation are solid communication skills. A good facilitator listens well, can synthesize different points being made and then repeat them back in an organized manner, involves others in the conversation, and is able to guide the conversation toward the goals.

There are many books and courses on effective facilitation that a project manager can research to build his or her skills. The best way to increase facilitation skills is through experience and practice. A project manager should watch successful facilitators to see how they run their meetings. A project manager might also consider finding a mentor who is a successful facilitator who can coach him or her on successful techniques. Lastly, asking for feedback from team members is a good way to get perspectives on how successful a facilitator the project manager is and some areas for development.

There are a few considerations that the project manager should pay special attention to as he or she gains experience in facilitation:

- Understanding group dynamics. Some resources are more vocal than others or have prior relationships that can affect their participation in the meeting. To have optimal outcomes, a project manager needs to obtain participation from the knowledgeable resources and not just the person who talks the most.
- Socialize key messages beforehand. In meetings with senior stakeholders where a project manager is trying to facilitate a decision, it is a good idea to socialize the information individually before the meeting. Sometimes when people see information for the first time, their reaction can be disruptive to the meeting (especially if it is bad news). Getting to those people before the meeting to understand how they will react will focus the meeting and help foster support for the agenda during the meeting.
- Stay on topic. Meetings tend to go in many different directions, and the use of a "parking lot" along with the acknowledgment of off-topic conversations will keep the focus on the agenda. The art of facilitating includes keeping the meeting on topic while not coming across as dismissive of people's contributions.
- Be conscious of verbal and nonverbal behavior. People rolling their eyes, becoming disengaged, or not interacting during the meeting can result in unsuccessful outcomes. The project manager needs to be cognizant of these signs and try to understand the reasons so that he or she can modify his or her approach.

4. Skill—Effective negotiation. Negotiation involves a group of two or more people with different goals working to find a mutually acceptable solution. The project manager spends a significant amount of

his or her time during the project on negotiation. Some examples include:

- Project scope and prioritization of work. When defining scope up front, projects usually have many stakeholders with overlapping agendas and competing priorities. The project manager needs to work with the team to make recommendations and find solutions to meet all of the stakeholder needs. This usually requires negotiating scope, activities, resources, and timelines.
- Change controls. As changes to scope get recognized, they are assessed for schedule and cost impact to the project and need to be agreed upon by the project sponsors. Negotiation is needed to accept the impacts of the change and still feel comfortable in the ability to meet updated project commitments.
- Resource acquisition. Project managers need to negotiate with resource managers for which resources they can get, when the resource can start, and the allocation of the resource that they can use on their project
- Issues and conflicts. There are always issues and conflicts that arise that the project manager must remediate. If those issues have impacts on the project commitments, then the project manager needs to facilitate getting the solution and negotiate the options with the project sponsors. Conflicts between resources also require effective negotiation because project team members need to continue to work together, so they must feel like the solution is acceptable to them.

There are several best practices that should be considered when a project manager is negotiating a situation:

- Negotiating requires planning. The objective needs to be clearly identified as well as constraints to the negotiation (e.g., time, money, resources, and technology constraints). Having data to support a position also helps because it keeps the negotiation focused on the facts.
- Stay away from blame by focusing on the issues. Negotiations can sometimes become personal and people can be viewed as being attacked. Facts and examples should be used rather than blame or accusations.
- Ask questions. If a project manager is negotiating a conflict between resources, asking questions is a good way to facilitate the conversation without being seen as authoritative. The conflict may require

a decision by the project manager, but starting with questions is a good way to gather information to make a balanced decision.

- Appropriate timing. The timing of a negotiation is important to the probability of a successful outcome. For example, if a resource has left a project and a new resource is needed, then immediate negotiation of the issue is appropriate. Conversely, if a heated argument between team members has taken place, it may make sense to wait until both parties have calmed down.
- Build alliances to gain support for the agenda. If the project manager is trying to negotiate support for an aspect of his or her project (e.g., increase in scope or a schedule extension), he or she may want to consider preselling the ideas to individuals that can be allies before having a meeting with the project sponsors.
- Understand styles and positions early. It may be helpful to keep a checklist of stakeholders and their styles and positions on specific areas. For example, knowing that a stakeholder likes to understand facts before making a decision will help the project manager prepare appropriately for the negotiation. Another example may be a stakeholder who only cares about the schedule of the project and may be more flexible on cost or scope.
- Use silence. Silence in meetings can be uncomfortable and people will usually start talking to fill in the spaces. This can be beneficial for people who like to speak as a way of gathering information.
- Make sure that people don't back down from their ideas when challenged. To avoid confrontation, sometimes people will back down from their ideas. A project manager should have people restate their position clearly to make sure that their perspective is being understood.

Negotiation is a difficult skill for some project managers because it is viewed as unpleasant and confrontational, but it is a critical skill needed for a consultative approach. To build these skills, a project manager can enroll in a training course that includes hands-on activities and case studies. This will provide a safe environment to try different techniques and styles to see what works best for that individual. Once the fundamentals of negotiation are understood, they can be applied to everyday situations, including ones outside of work to gain practical experience. Project managers should reflect on negotiations afterwards to understand why they were or were not successful and what can be changed the next time. Project managers might also want to consider using a professional negotiator on critical situations to have a neutral third party, and then observe their approach.

5. Skill—Listen and be seen as approachable. Listening is a fundamental skill for a project manager to have when using a consultative approach. While a project manager spends a significant amount of time communicating and presenting information, there are also many examples where it is important for them to listen effectively:

- Understanding the status of the project. Knowing the health of the project is important, and this comes directly from listening to team leads and team members as they provide status reports. The project manager needs to ask the right questions and understand underlying messages to properly gauge the status of the project.

- Understanding the impact of an issue, risk, or change. As items requiring attention get raised, the impacts of those items need to be fully recognized, as they may result in not meeting project commitments. To get this information, the project manager must successfully listen to many stakeholders who can determine the impacts.

- During conflicts and negotiations. Usually conflicts and negotiations have hidden agendas and personal feelings attached to them, so practicing effective listening is important to get to the root of the problem and have successful outcomes.

Effective communication is not about controlling the conversation and telling people what is important so much as understanding different viewpoints, the experience of team members, and personal feelings behind what people are saying. A project manager must be seen as approachable or critical project information will not be shared in a timely manner. There are several methods that a project manager can use to listen well to others:

- Show genuine interest and empathy. Try to understand where the speaker is coming from and his or her background with the topic. Pay specific attention to topics that the speaker is passionate about. Showing interest in what people have to say is an effective method of being seen as approachable. If team members do not feel like the project manager is approachable and listens to them, they will be less likely to share important information about the project, such as an upcoming risk or issue that requires action.

- Avoid distractions. In today's environment it is common for a meeting to have several people texting or checking e-mails in the room. It is worse for conference calls, where people are staring at their computers or having side conversations during the call. Showing interest means being engaged, looking attentively at the speaker, and acknowledging points verbally and nonverbally.

- Ask open-ended clarifying questions. If a topic is not clear or fully understood, a project manager should ask clarifying questions. Not only does this help to gain an understanding of the speaker's message and intent, but it also shows interest and builds credibility with the speaker.
- Paraphrase and summarize what others say. Repeating back a summary of the speaker shows understanding of the content and that he or she has been heard. This is also a good method for disagreements—to start with summarizing the other person's message and then present one's own opinion.
- Avoid interrupting. It is a common tendency to interrupt other people or not hear what they are saying because people are deciding their response before the person finishes speaking. This can be a result of many reasons, such as dismissing the other person because one feels that person does not know what he or she is talking about.
- Do not punish bad news. To be seen as approachable, a project manager must not react negatively to bad information. The result will be team members not sharing information, which will result in surprises later on in the project.

Like the other skills mentioned in this section, the best way to build effective listening skills is through practice and experience. Project managers should get feedback from their team members on how well they listen and how approachable they are. Once this feedback is received, they should consider the reasons that they behave in the manner that is perceived. They could be seen as dismissive of particular resources, not engaged, or not wanting to hear bad news. Effective listening skills can be applied outside of work so there are plenty of opportunities for practicing them.

Case Study: Influencing in a Matrixed Organization

Contributed by Vikas Bhor

I am a program manager at a large insurance company in Connecticut responsible for the delivery of a multi-million-dollar portfolio of projects. I work in a heavily matrixed organization with functional teams managed by resource managers and sourcing vendor partner resources spread across multiple countries. One of the biggest challenges that I face regularly is to get the appropriate level of support from all functional teams, resource managers, and vendor partners to ensure the smooth delivery of portfolio commitments.

In a matrixed organization, resource managers are primarily focused on developing the individual functional discipline, such as business analysts, technical leads, data modelers, and developers, in addition to supporting resourcing needs across projects and programs. We have multiple portfolios supporting different lines of business where resources are shared across the portfolios based on the demand and availability of resources with matching skill set. Vendor partners are focused on being the supply organization for functional roles such as developer and quality assurance. Vendor partners also have internal challenges to support resourcing demand across multiple clients.

Matrixed organizational structure causes competing and sometimes conflicting priorities between portfolio managers, project/program managers, resource managers, and vendor partners. In this environment, I have been using my influencing skills to get the support required from various teams to ensure smooth delivery of portfolio commitments.

Below are some of the key influencing techniques I use regularly:

1. Network with key stakeholders, including resource managers, team members, and vendor partners. Make an extra effort to know the key stakeholders and be genuinely interested in them. Keep key stakeholders engaged by inviting them to project kickoff meetings and celebrations of key milestones, involving them in key decisions as appropriate, including them in all key communications, and recognizing them for their support and assistance.
2. Everyone has a different working style and preference, so try and adapt to another person's working style as long as the other person is not bullying, taking advantage, or being unreasonable. Be cognizant of how people react to your style and continuously fine-tune the approach.
3. Actively and genuinely listen to other's concerns and issues, and be open to feedback from others. Also be open to share your concerns and issues and provide feedback. Take timely action on issues and concerns raised by others.
4. Be flexible and always try for a win-win solution. Partner with others to solve issues and share the ownership wherever appropriate. If an opportunity arises, go the extra mile to help others; it will start the cycle of helping each other for a mutually beneficial relationship.
5. Always keep difficult discussions fact based, spend extra time to collect facts, and articulate facts effectively.
6. Treat your sourcing vendor partners as part of your team. Show this by your deeds, not just words. Here is a simple example of what we did recently; after a major project release we sent a project celebration cake to our team located in India, in addition to having a celebration for the U.S. team.

7. Recognize good work in a timely manner and provide formal and informal feedback. This applies to sourcing vendor partner resources also. Spend time and resources celebrating major project milestones.
8. Schedule recurring one-on-one sessions with key stakeholders. This provides an excellent open forum for the stakeholder and PM to discuss issues, concerns, and solutions and share ideas.

Many of the above-mentioned influencing techniques may seem simple and logical, but I have personally seen many project, program, or portfolio managers fail or struggle to deliver due to a lack of understanding of and focus on the importance of influencing skills.

3.3.3 Self-Management

Having a focus on relationships and being influential are essential to using a consultative approach to project management. To take these skills to the next level of effectiveness requires self-awareness and self-management. These are the main characteristics of a concept called emotional intelligence (EI). Emotional intelligence describes the ability, capacity, skill, or in the case of the EI model, trait—a self-perceived ability to identify, assess, and manage the emotions of one's self, of others, and of groups (Bradberry et al., 2005).

In 1998, Daniel Goleman expanded upon emotional intelligence in the workplace by demonstrating that just having raw intelligence or emotional intelligence is not enough to be successful as a professional. He introduces the concept of emotional competence. "Our emotional intelligence determines our potential for learning the practical skills that are based on its five elements: self-awareness, motivation, self-regulation, empathy and adeptness at relationships. Our emotional competence shows how much of that potential we have translated into on-the-job capabilities" (Goleman, 1998).

In his book, Goleman described an emotional competency model that has five key components (Goleman, 1998, page 24):

1. Self-awareness—Knowing one's emotions and recognizing their impact on others.
2. Self-regulation—Managing and controlling one's self.
3. Self-motivation—Striving for excellence in one's work.
4. Empathy—Being aware of others' feelings and concerns.
5. Social skills—Creating desirable responses in others.

Each of the components are important for project managers to understand, use, and improve upon as they relate directly to their ability to influence the teams and stakeholders for desired results in the new project landscape. Table 3.4 relates these components of emotional competence to project management examples.

Of the techniques and skills mentioned in this book, building emotional competencies is the hardest because they build on the core characteristics of a person's personality, interpersonal style, and habits. They usually require a conscious effort to recognize and a constant effort to improve and change.

3.3.3.1 Techniques and Skills

1. Skill—Self-awareness. At the core of self-management is recognizing the impacts of one's words and actions on others around him or her. For project managers this translates into how effective they are at influencing stakeholders, managing conflicts, and motivating project team members. There are two key components to self-awareness:
   a. Understanding one's self
   b. Recognizing the effect of one's words and actions on others

   First, a project manager needs to be aware of his or her strengths, limitations, responses to situations, and motivators. There are several reasons why this is important:

   - Knowing strengths that a project manager can use to be successful in specific situations. For example, a project manager may be really good at organizing information and can leverage that skill to keep the project well run.
   - Being aware of limitations where an expert, coach, or mentor can help the project manager. In the example above, that same project manager may not have effective communication skills. Therefore, he or she has an organized plan, but plan activities are not clear. In this example, a project manager can seek advice from a mentor or bring in a communications specialist to complement his or her skills.
   - Understanding why a certain situation causes a person stress is important so that he or she can identify that situation and plan/act accordingly. For example, if a project manager does not like conflict, he or she may shy away from escalating bad news. Consciously recognizing that as a stressful situation the project manager avoids can help him or her create an approach to better managing those situations.

TABLE 3.4

Emotional Competence in Project Management

Competency	Project Management Examples
Self-awareness	• Recognizing the effects of decisions made, personal management style, and interaction with project team members and stakeholders • Understanding one's strengths and utilizing them in maximizing influence and outcomes • Understanding one's limitations so peers, team members, and experts can be used optimally to support him or her • Self-confidence to stand up for project commitments, raise issues, and lead the team
Self-regulation	• Controlling one's self to stay focused on the tasks and set a positive example for the team • Taking accountability for the performance of the project • Being flexible with different approaches and styles of the project team members
Self-motivation	• Showing commitment for the project goals and confidence in meeting them • Taking initiative to follow up on open items and looking for improvement opportunities
Empathy	• Understanding the perspectives of project team members and stakeholders • Appreciating the feelings and concerns of project team members • Recognizing customer needs and focusing on meeting them • Being aware of cultural and political nuances
Social skills	• Communicating effectively • Being a champion of change • Being able to inspire and motivate teams of people

- Recognizing bad habits, such as interrupting people, dismissing different opinions, rolling one's eyes, or showing up late to meetings, can help a project manager make a concerted effort to modify these behaviors that have negative consequences on his or her relationship with the team and stakeholders.

There are a few techniques that a project manager can use to improve his or her ability to be self-aware:

- Introspection. Make time to write down strengths, limitations, motivators, and stressful situations. Consider why certain situations are motivators and others are viewed as stressful, and then document a thoughtful action plan as to how to respond to each specific situation.
- Take a self-assessment. There are many personality and style assessments in the marketplace that show leadership styles, such as the Myers–Briggs and DISC. These can be used to generate insights into management style and relationships to other personality styles. These assessments also typically have approaches and best practices for interacting with different personality styles.
- Get feedback. Ask for specific feedback from peers, managers, and team members around management style and work habits. Try not to debate the feedback, as it is that person's opinion, and therefore there is probably some truth to it. Thank him or her for the feedback and then consider why he or she may have those perceptions.

Building on self-awareness, project managers must then recognize how their words and actions are contributing to their ability to influence team members and stakeholders. Not all situations are the same. A project manager needs to be aware of his or her personality style, how effectively he or she interacts in a situation, and then adjust his or her approach based on that recognition. There are several ways to recognize impacts:

- Watch verbal and nonverbal cues. Pay attention to people's faces and posture during meetings and conversations.
- Reflect on interactions. After an interaction with people, reflect on the outcomes of the interaction and consider what worked and what did not work. Think of alternatives that could have been used in those situations.
- Ask for feedback. This will enable a project manager to gain insights into the perception that others have of him or her during situations.

2. Skill—Self-regulation. Once project managers are aware of their style and its impacts on others, they should work on controlling how they respond to situations. There are several techniques that a project manager can use to do this:

- Slow down and not respond automatically. During a conversation, negotiation, or critical issue, pause and think about the best response to the situation. The initial knee-jerk reaction may be an emotional response instead of a logical response, and may result in less than optimal outcomes (such as damaging a relationship or straining a reputation that took a long time to build).

- Stay composed and focused. It is important for project managers to keep their composure because the team is looking to them for direction, confidence, and motivation. Staying focused on the facts of the situation and not being impulsive will increase credibility with the project team and gain their confidence.

- Consider consequences. During an interaction, it is important to understand the consequences of a project manager's comments or actions. For example, a project manager may be frustrated that a resource manager has pulled a critical resource on his or her team and may want to yell at that resource manager. While that may make the PM feel a little better in the short term, it may result in the long-term problem of not getting good resources from that manager on future projects.

- Create new habits and practice them. Habits are hard to break, but they must be recognized and worked on constantly in order to improve. For example, bad meeting etiquette will continue to result in suboptimal results and give a project manager a bad reputation. Team members sometimes have influence over which projects they want to work on, and if they know that a particular project manager is rude and dismissive, then they may choose to not work on his or her project.

3. Skill—Self-motivation. Demonstrating motivation is an important way for a project manager to influence the project team and stakeholders. People do not want to work for a project manager who doesn't seem interested in the success of the project or like he or she even wants to be there. Project members can pick up on this very quickly, and it does affect their motivation and desire for working on the project.

Project managers should understand what motivates them and then look for opportunities to work on those types of engagements. If there is not flexibility in work assignments, the project manager should identify something about the project that excites him or her. Examples of project characteristics that typically motivate project managers are:

- Sense of accomplishment. Completing a project within the given constraints is a very satisfying feeling because of the sense of accomplishment and recognition that comes with that.
- Challenges. Some project managers like working on challenging projects, which can be new technologies that have not been used at the company before, implementing a new business process that will change how business is done, or working on a project with aggressive commitments.
- Working with people. Some project managers enjoy the aspect of coordinating many different people toward a common goal.
- Visibility. Working on a project that has a lot of management visibility can be viewed as a good thing for people's careers (assuming it goes well).

Another component of self-motivation is demonstrating commitment to the project. By taking action on open items and following up on behalf of the team, a project manager can gain credibility with the team, who will be more likely to help him or her meet project commitments. Positive motivation and commitment can be seen as contagious— and so can negative commitment. The project manager should not undervalue how influential his or her own motivation is to the other members of the project team.

4. Skill—Empathy. Another important component of self-management is showing empathy toward project team members and stakeholders. The essence of empathy is putting oneself in another's shoes. This means listening to that person's perspectives, opinions, and concerns and trying to understand where he or she is coming from. Sometimes project managers act as counsel to team members who bring their emotions and interject them into work. They need to recognize that being empathetic is part of their ability to influence the team. A project manager demonstrating that he or she is genuinely interested in the team members and their perspectives and how they feel will increase people's willingness to share information and experiences with the project manager, resulting in better project

outcomes. It also strengthens the relationship between the team and the project manager.

In his very successful book *The Seven Habits of Highly Effective People*, Stephen Covey (1989) described the concept of empathetic communication in his Habit 5, entitled "Seek First to Understand." The concept is to take the time to really understand the situation and where another person is coming from before reacting or responding. Specifically when communicating with people, this requires focusing on what the other person is saying and trying to understand his or her frame of reference. "Most people do not listen with the intent to be understood; they listen with the intent to reply. They're either speaking or preparing to speak" (Covey, 1989, page 239).

There are a few ways that project managers can become more empathetic:

- Put themselves in someone else's shoes. Consider the experiences and feelings of others in a particular situation. For example, a team member may have had a bad experience with project managers in the past and is therefore reluctant to raise issues that they know will harm the project.
- Acknowledge other people's feelings and opinions. During facilitated sessions or individual meetings, project managers can acknowledge differing opinions by stating them back verbally or nodding their heads. Project managers should also be careful not to be seen as dismissive of other people's input (e.g., "I understand your concern, but here is what I want …").
- Ask questions to gain understanding. This shows interest in the other person and his or her perspectives. The project manager should let the team member respond and present his or her opinions fully without showing judgment.

5. Skill—Social skills. Having social skills speaks to how well a project manager relates to his or her project stakeholders and team and is able to influence their behaviors to produce a successful outcome. There are several characteristics included in social skills, all of which are covered in detail in other sections of this book:

Building relationships. Section 3.3.1 reviewed techniques concerning building and fostering relationships to effectively influence others and gather critical information.

Having influence. Techniques and skills were discussed in Section 3.3.2. This includes negotiation, facilitation, and effective listening.

Effective communication skills. Section 3.4 will cover effective communication techniques and skills.

Being seen as approachable so that team members feel like they
can raise issues or concerns in real time, before they become
bigger problems.

Creating bonds with people and being seen as genuine, capable,
and approachable are important to the consultative approach and,
in many ways, more effective than having good fundamental project
management skills.

Case Study: Oblivious to Reactions of Others

Contributed by Kerry Wills

The best case that I can think of for self-management is a case of what not
to do, as opposed to a case of someone who is very self-aware. This case
is of an individual who was a manager in a company that I worked for as
a consultant. He was not aware of how his actions and words affected the
people around him. We were working on a multi-million-dollar project and
I had been at the company for several years. This individual was brought in
as the business lead for the project.

There are several examples of his style of management and interaction
with the team that demonstrate his interactions and the impact:

- The way he talked to people. This individual was perceived as arrogant because he seemed to talk down to the team in almost every
  conversation. This resulted in people not wanting to meet with him
  and subject themselves to his tirades and rants.
- Lack of trust. This individual spent a significant amount of his time
  checking our work. The best example that I vividly remember was
  one day when the team was accused of charging too many expenses.
  Another example was when we stayed late and ordered in food
  (which was the policy for staying beyond 6 p.m.); he was convinced
  that we would order extra meals and bring them home. He also com-
  mented on when we ordered office supplies that we could have just
  "brought pens from home" to use. The lack of trust was unfounded,
  incorrect, and demoralizing to the team. The irony was that we were
  working on a multi-million-dollar program, and instead of spending
  time making sure that we would meet our commitments, he was
  looking at expense receipts for pens and dinners.
- Micromanaging the team. He also micromanaged the work on the
  team and was constantly asking for technical details well beyond
  what his role should have interest in. This individual did not have any

background in the technologies that we used, so most of the time we were explaining to him how the solution worked. This was also time that was taken away from the work that we needed to do (which is why we had to stay late and order dinners a lot). It also continued to show a lack of trust for the team, our experience, and the work that we were doing.

- Lack of empathy. Because we were consultants and on a fixed fee, this person showed no empathy for the amount of work that we had to do to meet commitments. He was always trying to add more scope to the project, knowing that his company would not have to pay more for it.
- Would not interact with the team. We had several team events, and the few that he did attend he would not engage with the team. I remember one dinner in particular where he came with his wife and actually sat at a separate table than the rest of the team. He also seemed to be uncomfortable in social settings and with talking to people about topics that were not related to work.

The net result of this individual's interactions with the team is that people did not want to have meetings with him, ask for his feedback, or show him our progress. The fear was that they would be criticized, micromanaged, or have to spend large amounts of time explaining concepts that were not relevant to the conversion.

This individual seemed oblivious to the way he was coming across to people in meetings or in social settings. This is evident in the fact that he continued to behave in the way explained above and did not change his style based on the responses that he was getting from the project team.

3.3.4 Political Savvy

At the apex of the consultative approach is being politically savvy. These are people who understand their organizations, can identify who the key players are, and know what is needed to successfully navigate the company. There are several common characteristics of people who are politically savvy within an organization:

- They manage to consistently get things done despite obstacles that arise and organizational barriers.
- They recognize the impacts of decisions and trends on their work and other areas within the organization.
- They are able to accurately predict what organizations and individuals will do in certain situations.
- They seem to always select the right approach for situations.

Because of the increasing number of stakeholders and organizations involved in projects, it is very important for project managers to improve their ability to be politically savvy. This is no longer just a skill needed for senior leaders.

3.3.4.1 Techniques and Skills

1. Technique—Understand the organization. The first step in being politically savvy is to understand the entire organization that the project is working in. This allows the project manager to identify the key players, know what divisions perform what functions, and see the context of the project. There are several ways to get this understanding:
   - Know the structure. Have the organization chart memorized. Knowing the purpose of each organization and who the leaders are is important for context, especially when they show up to meetings.
   - Know the players. Once the organization chart is known, focus on learning who the influential players are in each division. These are the people that the project manager will need to obtain support from or who could easily set up obstacles that will impact the project. Create a list of the go-to people for each organization.
   - Know the processes. Each organization has its own set of processes and rules. Being aware of these will help the project manager to navigate properly and be successful in working with that area.
   - Know the culture. Having an awareness of the cultural habits, themes, and "land mines" will help the project manager to work with the organization and avoid pitfalls that could stall the project.
2. Technique—Develop coalitions. Once there is an awareness of the organization, the project manager should then look to create a coalition of allies. This builds on the relationship focus discussed earlier in this chapter. Beyond just having relationships with key stakeholders, the politically savvy project manager has support from them as well. There are several ways that a coalition can be built on a project:
   - Focus on the right people. "It's not what you know, but who you know" is a relevant quote in reference to project managers. The

coalitions should be people who can directly influence the project work. The following people should be considered in the coalition:

- Managers of key resources who can be leveraged to obtain skilled resources on the project.
- Shared service resources that manage key portions of the project and have competing priorities.
- Leaders who can help to get decisions made quickly. These are people who can also back up the project manager at important meetings where decisions need to be made.
- Team members who are vocal (informal leaders). Most projects have team members with resources who have been at the company for a long time and have a lot of informal leadership and credibility within the organization. Getting these people to be part of the coalition and visibly committed to the project is critical to the success of the project.

- Build the coalition. Once the right people are identified, the project manager should look to build the bond. Several techniques were listed earlier regarding how to build relationships. One effective method is to set up regular informal meetings (possibly over lunch). These can then be used to gather advice or ask for help. The project manager needs to work with his or her allies to agree upon approaches and positions so that they are "on the same page" and can get support when he or she needs it.

Coalitions are important, but there is a risk of being perceived as playing on the "wrong" team. Organizational politics are always changing, and being seen as connected to people who are losing political favorability can have negative results. A project manager will need to be astute as to changing tides of the organization and with whom he or she is aligned.

3. Technique—Observe others. One of the best ways to build political skills is to watch others and their effectiveness at using different techniques. A project manager should observe people who are good at "playing the game" to see what they are doing and how they do it. Also, be cognizant of people who are not successful to understand their mistakes and the results of them. Watching people succeed and fail in an organization will help the project manager learn the values and culture of an organization. Plus, he or she can learn from others' mistakes, as opposed to learning the hard way and repeating them.

4. Skill—Know personal style of politics. Watching others is helpful to see what styles work, but the project manager has to use an approach that is genuine to his or her own nature, or it will not be effective. This relates to the self-awareness skills listed earlier in this chapter. A project manager should be aware of his or her personal styles and use an approach that is comfortable for him or her. For example, if a project manager is not very social or gregarious, then it may not be natural for him or her to interact on a social basis. He or she might want to consider building allies based on a common interest in work areas, such as a belief in process rigor or a shared professional goal.

5. Skill—Be viewed as politically savvy vs. political. To be successful, a project manager needs to be viewed as being politically savvy and not political. Having a reputation as acting manipulative or sneaky will impact the project manager's ability to influence others and motivate the team for success. In order to be viewed as successful in organization politics, a project manager should focus on the following recommendations:

- Demonstrate behaviors. A project manager needs to exhibit honesty, trust, and integrity at all times. The project team is constantly watching what the project manager does and says, and if they do not believe that the PM is genuine, then it will be very hard to build back that trust and get commitment.
- Change style for situation. Based on the situation and people involved, the project manager may need to adopt their political style. For example, sometimes it is best to discuss challenges head on, and sometimes it is better to not immediately react and to let things play out.
- Consider implications. Coalitions should not be based on mutual dislike of individuals. Discussing someone else in a negative manner is dangerous because there is always the possibility of that conversation coming back to the person. This can significantly change the support received for the project.

Case Study: Savvy with Executives and Admired by the People

Contributed by Kerry Wills

As a consultant, I have worked in many organizations that all had unique corporate cultures. I had worked with one chief information officer (CIO) in particular who was very politically savvy. I respected the way in which he could successfully navigate the organization and still not come across as arrogant, political, or sneaky. He was also well liked by the organization and respected by his business customers. He was not the typical CIO, and that is what made him successful.

His style of leadership and savvy can be described in a few ways:

- Building relationships and coalitions. This CIO spent a lot of time fostering relationships and coalitions across the entire organization on both the IT and business side. It seemed he had lunch with a different person every day.
- Knowing the organization. Based on the relationships that he had built, he knew how to steer his way through the organization and who to contact when he needed anything. This was useful during conflicts or challenges where an escalation with a rapid response was needed.
- Knowing the people. As busy as he was running the organization, he always found time to walk the floor and talk to the people. This, combined with his sense of humor and approachable style, made him a favorite leader in the organization. The result of this respect and admiration was that he had people who would willingly work for him and do what was requested.
- Being cognizant of the politics. While the CIO spent a lot of time on building relationships, he also had a good understanding of the personalities of the executives and associated politics between them. This information helped him to coach his leadership team on the best way to interact with the other executives.
- Being seen as approachable. The down-to-earth manner that this CIO presented made it easy for people to approach him and share information. This meant that he was always "in the know" as to what was going on in the organization. This also contributed to his effectiveness at being savvy.

This CIO had the rare combination of being politically savvy with the executives in the organization and also being likeable to the people within the organization. It is too often that executives only manage up and with their peers and think that their title is enough to motivate their own organizations. This CIO actually cared and came across as genuine.

When I think of being politically savvy, I think of this individual and how he was able to navigate the personalities of the organization and deal with the politics while at the same time keeping the respect and loyalty of his organization.

3.4 MANAGING INFORMATION

The need for effective communication and transparent information is pervasive across all aspects of the new project landscape. In order for project managers to be successful, there must be multiple levels of communication as well as constant visibility of relevant information. Project communication is not only about status reports and management presentations, but also about getting the right information to the right people at the right time. Examples of information needs in a typical project include:

- Communication of status. Stakeholders need to understand where the project stands in relation to commitments. This includes activities completed, upcoming milestones, and any items that require attention.
- Escalation of issues, risks, or change that can have an impact on the project commitments. These need to be documented properly, including a clear description of the challenge, impacts, and options/recommendations.
- Interactions with vendors or stakeholders. Because of the increasing number of touch points, keeping all projects stakeholders coordinated requires constant communication around next steps and project needs. This can include confirming resource availability, following up on project plan activities, and obtaining input from stakeholders.
- Project goals and context. Team members get very focused on their specific activities and lose focus on the big picture. The project manager needs to continually communicate the vision, approach, and plan to the team members to keep them focused and at the same time aware of the overall progress and goals.

Figure 3.8 highlights the three key steps in project communication: communication planning, the gathering of information, and the presenting of information. These steps are cyclical in that the

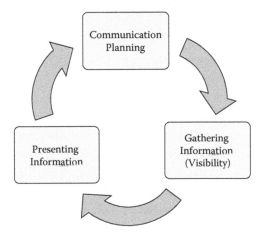

FIGURE 3.8
Project communication steps.

planning, gathering, and presenting of information are continual during a project and not one-time activities.

Like the other aspects described in the book, project communication techniques and skills require an investment in time and a concerted effort to utilize effectively. They also require practice and experience to utilize optimally.

3.4.1 Proper Communications Planning

Project communication needs to be recognized as an important aspect to the project that requires time spent up front in planning. Because of the increasing complexity of projects, a project manager has many moving parts and stakeholders that require information to help the project meet its commitments. Making an early investment in stakeholder analysis and communication planning will help the project manager to have a solid approach for managing the information between these moving parts.

3.4.1.1 Techniques and Skills

1. Technique—Create a communication plan. Creating a communication plan is an important component to a project's success. Ineffective communication can result in delayed decisions, rework due to stakeholders not getting information early, differences in expectations, low morale, and missed commitments. A communication plan should be created early in the project and followed throughout the life of the project.

   There are several considerations when a project manager is creating a project communication plan:
   - Determine the objectives of the communication plan. These can include providing status updates, reminding people of upcoming activities, or getting management visibility for the project. An objective might also be to document key decisions or risks should they be questioned at a later point (i.e., "covering one's rear").
   - Inventorying the stakeholders who require communication and what information they need. Stakeholders can include team members, management, other divisions, managers of project resources, and vendors. Each stakeholder may require different information, so it is important to consider (and document) each. For example,

management may want to see progress and any impending challenges. Team members may want to understand upcoming work and knowledge of work on other parts of the project.

- Identify the format of communications. There are many ways that a project can communicate information, which are listed below. A project manager needs to identify the best format for communicating information given the stakeholders and type of information being communicated.

  - Executive summaries or management briefings usually include bullets of high-level summaries on the project's progress as well as items for management attention called out. These are best used to send out to senior leaders who have a stake in the project and need to understand the status, but not at a detailed level.

  - Presentations are used to highlight key points of a project or tell a particular story. Visuals can be used to accentuate key points. Presentations are usually made to a specific audience with a specific agenda. For example, "lunch and learn" sessions can be used to share specific project information with stakeholders in an informal setting.

  - Status reports are generally used to identify accomplishments, activities planned for the next period, and also note any open issues or risks. Status reports usually get distributed to a wide audience.

  - Newsletters can be used to bring attention to a project's goals and accomplishments. Newsletters are sent to a wide audience and are effective ways of marketing the project with such focus areas as customer interviews or personal stories.

  - Webinars are becoming popular means to demonstrate functionality and provide "buzz" for a project.

  - Project meetings are common ways to communicate status and to have a regular forum for raising items that need action. These can include project steering committee meetings or project team status meetings.

- Determine frequency of communications. Not all stakeholders need information at the same time, which needs to be considered when creating the communication plan. For example, team members and direct project stakeholders need information more frequently than managers of project resources.

- Identification of the information source. Some information may come from project tools and some may be more anecdotal. It is important to understand where "the truth" lies for information, so the wrong information is not reported on. For example, project financial information may come from finance as opposed to being calculated separately by the project team.

2. Technique—Plan to get the team into a cadence for information. An important part of communication planning is consideration for the project team and how they receive information. The project manager should look to have regular meetings with the project team to share information and collaborate. This provides a cadence to the project, where the team members come to expect information at specific times. A well-run team meeting provides many benefits:

   - Team members know that information will be shared at a specific time every week and can plan their schedules around that meeting.
   - Team members are aware that concerns and challenges can be raised in this forum and discussed.
   - Preparing for the status meeting becomes a habit of the team.
   - Focusing beyond explaining status and more on forward-looking planning and proactive issues and risk management.

   Having this rhythm allows the project team to understand expectations and consistently work toward them. For example, they know that at every team meeting they are expected to present their status and progress on open actions and issues. Rescheduling these meetings should be kept to a minimum to avoid disrupting the flow. The next part of this section discusses other ways to get information, but having a regular status meeting is the foundation from which the other techniques can be built.

Case Study: Good Planning but Then "Communica-shun"

Contributed by Kerry Wills

I was running a change program for a Fortune 500 company that had many stakeholders from different areas of the company that would be impacted by the outcomes. It was therefore extremely important to make sure that we planned for communications properly. I had assigned a team lead in charge of communications, and together we created a comprehensive communications plan.

There were several components to the communications plan. We identified all of the stakeholders that would be impacted by the project and included them in a list. We then considered the key messages and forums by which to communicate to each stakeholder. We also identified several methods by which we would communicate the project. We used webinars for large groups of people, team meetings for more intimate discussions, and monthly newsletters to communicate progress. We also kept a running log of all communications and meetings, when they were and who attended.

Even with all of the communications planning, we still had many challenges in the execution of that plan. The two main challenges that we had with communications were with acceptance by the people who had to embrace the change and having management support for the project.

PEOPLE WEREN'T READY

Even though we sent out newsletters and went to every team meeting and forum in the organization over a three-month period, there were still many people who were not aware of the activities within the project. This astounded us, but we realized that mass messages to people or even meetings would not be effective if people did not think that the outcomes of the project would have an impact on their jobs. We were also communicating activities several months in advance, so the timing of the messages may not have been optimal because there were no impending changes.

MANAGEMENT SUPPORT

The bigger issue that we had was that there was not full management support of the project or the use of its deliverables. While we were invited to team meetings to present the materials, some of the same senior leaders who ran those meetings were not major supporters of the project and its objectives. It is very hard to champion any kind of change program when there is not full and consistent management support. I view this as a "sponsorship-wreck." It is worth noting that since the inception of the project there were some management changes (including the project sponsor), senior people leaving, and a lot of economic uncertainty around the company.

I realized the lack of support on one very unforgettable day. Our team had been putting out high-quality newsletters to the organization with photos, quotes, and metrics that identified the key aspects and progress of the project. I had been discussing the project with a senior executive who told me that the newsletter "looked too professional" and gave the perception that we were spending too much time making fancy newsletters and not enough time on executing the outcomes of the project. I found this ironic since it is hard to deploy a change initiative without clear and frequent communications. The net result is that we essentially stopped communicating to stakeholders altogether.

CONCLUSIONS

I learned many important lessons from this change project about communication planning beyond just having a solid communications plan. The first is to make sure that the messages are relevant, timely, and important for the audience. The "what's in it for me" has to be clear and significant in order for people to listen. The second lesson I learned is to make sure that there is full leadership support for the initiative before starting the communication process; otherwise, it has the risk of being ineffective.

3.4.2 Gathering Information: Visibility

Visibility is the ability of the project manager to gather, understand, and be able to clearly articulate relevant and timely information. A project will have a hard time being successful if the project manager does not have timely information to manage the progress of the plan or is not aware of critical risks or issues. For example, there is a common project situation where a resource week after week says that they are on track and continues to report that they are at 80% complete. Then comes the day of delivery and they say that they won't be done for a few more weeks and that they had been saying this all along. This is one example of why communication is important, but is flawed without visibility of relevant information.

There are many ways to gather information and achieve visibility into a project. A project manager must plan to spend part of his or her day understanding the status of activities and any potential risks or issues. There also needs to be an environment of trust such that if a team member is behind on his or her work, he or she feels comfortable raising the issue to the project manager without fear of reprise.

3.4.2.1 Techniques and Skills

1. Technique—Collect the right information. A project manager has to collect information from many different aspects of the project to understand its health:
   - Progress toward the plan. This includes status of activities, progress toward key milestones, and starting activities when scheduled. Gathering this information usually requires going to multiple sources of information and people.
   - Resources. Understanding which resources are joining and leaving the project and the associated timing. Any resources that are

joining the project need to be planned for properly so they can be effective when they join.

- Identification of issues, risks, and challenges to the project and any associated impacts to the project's goals. Once identified, appropriate information needs to be gathered to determine the magnitude of the impact, and any recommendations or decisions assessed that need to be made by management.
- Financial information. Collecting data on actual spend to date and forecasted spend remaining. This information comes from several sources and usually involves some financial analysis to determine trending and forecasting.
- Risks to delivery. Project risks can come from any aspect of the project, and the project manager needs to understand where they are and be able to monitor them closely so they don't evolve into major problems on the project.

Information is usually collected from project resources, project management tools, and project documentation. The project manager must sort through the data and understand what they mean to the project so that he or she can accurately reflect the key messages or escalate items for management attention. As part of the project communication planning, the project manager should have identified the appropriate method and format for communicating project information as well as its source.

2. Technique—Management by walking around (MBWA). Management by walking around is an approach whereby the project manager walks around to the team members and has informal conversations with them on work-related topics. MBWA is a great technique for genuinely interacting with the team, establishing their trust, and getting qualitative information on the project. It shows interest in people and what they are doing and results in information gathering significantly quicker than any status meeting can. For projects with team members not located with them, it is a little harder to do, but a project manager can still use phone calls or instant messages.

There are a few key points for using the MBWA technique.

- Talk to all team members. Project managers spend regular time with their team leads but probably not as much with the team members working for the leads. These are the people doing most of the work, so it is important to get their perspectives. The project manager should also talk to as many team members as possible to avoid a perception of favoritism and only spending time with certain people.

- Be careful of supervisor relationships. The project manager needs to respect the reporting relationship on the project and avoid giving direction that may trump that of the team leads. Project managers should direct team members to their supervisors when these situations arise.
- It needs to be one on one. To personalize the conversation, it should be with the individual and not in a group. Team members may not be so forthcoming with information in larger settings.
- Ask questions. Asking probing questions shows interest in the team members' work and is a valuable way to understand the work, status, and challenges.
- Recognize timing. If there is a deadline coming or a team member looks particularly stressed, it may not be the best time to stop by.

MBWA is one of the most effective methods of obtaining information early in a project. Even if it means attending less project meetings, project managers should block off time on their calendar and make it a priority and a regular activity. Information gathered in a fifteen-minute floor conversation is usually more relevant and timely than information presented in most status meetings.

3. Skill—Create an environment of trust. Trust is critically important to ensure that resources feel comfortable raising issues as they happen or risks before they come to fruition. MBWA will not work without a sense of comfort and trust with the project manager. Demonstrating trust also yields benefits of increased productivity, as Ralph Waldo Emerson states: "Trust men and they will be true to you; treat them greatly and they will show themselves great."

There are several ways to create an environment of trust:

- Demonstrate integrity. The project manager should always act with integrity and the highest standards because team members are watching him or her. People will not want to do their best work for a project manager that they don't respect.
- Be approachable. Being seen as approachable is important so team members feel that they can bring the project manager real-time information. If a team member feels that the project manager doesn't want to hear his or her concerns, then he or she is less likely to bring them up, which makes the risks more likely to happen.

- Be available. Being seen as approachable is not useful if the project manager is not available. Like a college professor, a project manager may want to have known "office hours" so team members can stop by.
- Do not punish bad news. Overreacting to bad news is the worst thing that a project manager can do regarding having trust from the team. No one will want to raise issues in an environment of blame and punishment.

Case Study: The Agile Art of Visibility

Contributed by Randy Wills

This case study will focus on the importance of visibility of information on a project to increase the chances of success. The project was a multiyear system conversion to consolidate all websites into a single technology for agents, insureds, and call center resources. The project was managed using the extreme programming (xP) methodology, which is a derivative of the agile software development methodology. This case study is not intended to provide an overview of agile, but of the key components that provide visibility of information and the benefits gained because of them. Readers are encouraged to take the portions of this case study that make sense in the context in which they are working and then fashion them into their own projects regardless of delivery methodology used.

I was a resource manager at an insurance company in the Midwest managing a large system conversion effort using an agile software development approach. I was managing three concurrent teams working toward revising the company's customer websites. Each team was handling a single piece of functionality, such as adding a vehicle, changing address, adding a driver, billing, etc. Even though the teams had independent pieces of functionality, they all had to work together to coordinate programming, testing, and defects since all three teams were working in the same technical environment. This required a lot of coordination by the project manager and team members to ensure that there were synergy and good teamwork. The project had many moving pieces, so gathering information on the project as early as possible was critical to keep it moving.

There are certain activities in the agile methodology that are geared at increasing visibility of information on a project. Visibility can mean many things, all of which are important in moving the needle closer to a project's success:

- Visibility of scope. The business working more closely with IT to move away from the "that's what I said" vs. "that's what I heard" vs. "that's what I meant" common conundrum.

- Visibility of status. Management understanding the true progress and status of the project (i.e., moving away from the same 90% complete status for three weeks straight and more toward the real state of the project).
- Visibility of challenges. Identifying issues and risks early on to avoid fire drills by acting on them quickly.
- Visibility of resources. Understanding the resource skill sets, which allows for the ability to manage resources appropriately.
- Visibility of quality. Moving toward developers having more accountability for the quality of their work vs. having testers find their mistakes.

The agile methodology has many different techniques to help address the above-stated items. A few of these are mentioned below to help provide examples of steps that were taken to increase the project's visibility internally and with the business customer.

CO-LOCATION

It is difficult in today's multilocation, multicountry, work-from-home workforce environments, but when appropriate, it makes sense to have the entire team (including the business partners) sitting in the same location. For the system consolidation effort, the business customer initially had resistance to sitting with the IT team, but due to the importance, size, and necessity to "get it right," the business eventually agreed. This was an important step, as now the business was truly committed to the project. This enabled the IT team to see, hear, and experience the business as part of the project, and not just the resource that comes in, tells you the requirements, and then isn't heard from again until testing, when it is discovered that the requirements aren't what they meant. This partnership was the cornerstone for the entire project team to be successful. As questions, concerns, and risks came up, they were handled immediately, as opposed to waiting for e-mails to be read or not asking the question. It also allowed the IT project team to have more face time with their business partners to see and hear what they are working on. Co-location provided visibility from the business into the day-to-day workings of the IT project team, and for the IT project team to see, hear, and feel what the business worked on and what the project was looking to achieve.

THE DAILY STAND-UP MEETING

Every morning the entire project team would stand up for fifteen minutes and each person would say what he or she did yesterday, what he or she plans for today, and any issues. The intent of having everyone stand up was so it would go by faster. This was not intended to be a long status, but to have the project team hear what others are working on. Oftentimes during the system consolidation, if a developer was stuck on something, someone else on the team had a similar problem. It was common during the stand-up meeting for someone to mention what he or she was struggling with and someone else to chime in and mention that he or she also had that issue and they would work together after the meeting to resolve it. This greatly improved team communication, allowed for team members to grow, and increased efficiency, as oftentimes the developers would spend hours trying to figure out a problem that someone else could help them resolve in a matter of minutes. The daily stand-up meeting provided visibility from within the team on who was working on what, what people were struggling with, and who needed help.

TEST-DRIVEN DEVELOPMENT

One of the tenants of agile is automated testing. This entailed the developer to build its own automated tests, which were then added to a pool of automated tests. When the developer was ready with its piece of programming, it would run the full suite of tests. Only if the full suite of tests passed would it then be passed off to the testing team. The intent of this was to provide visibility to the developers of whether what they developed worked correctly *and* didn't break what was previously built by the team. Too often when a project is squeezed for time, quality goes out the window. This extra step forces the developer to ensure that the quality is there before the team tests every possible scenario. The developers on the system conversion team at first didn't feel this was their responsibility, but over time they came to understood that for the benefit of the entire project, this step was needed. This allowed the testing team to focus on testing all of the areas and not waste time logging defects and following up on some poor-quality items that the developer rushed to provide. Visibility and ownership are put back on the developers, in this case, to ensure that what they are producing is the best quality it can be before moving on to the next piece of work.

SHOW AND TELLS

At the end of every two weeks, the team would prepare for a "show and tell" meeting with the business sponsors and leadership team. This allowed the business sponsors to actually see what was programmed and the associated metrics of the team. All too often the business sponsors and leaders don't see a product until the project is in the testing phase, and this runs a high risk of not meeting expectations. At the end of every two weeks our project team would have the business analyst and business subject matter experts demonstrate, via a laptop and project, what the project had achieved for those prior two weeks. This allowed the business and project leadership team to see, provide feedback, and understand the progress that was made during that two-week cycle. Visibility into the project's progress, any issues, key metrics, and having the business team present it helped foster better business-IT cohesion and address any questions early on in the project life cycle.

RETROSPECTIVES

Many projects have postproject reviews, where it is discussed what could be done better. What the project team did was to follow the agile approach of retrospectives every two weeks where the project team (without management) would get together and draw on the whiteboard what went well and what didn't during last two weeks. Some of the items that the project team wrote down were things like "we could better work with the business if we had wireless so that we could move our laptops around without trying to find a connection" and "it's great having the business sit with us, but we would like to ask for specific office hours when we can know that they won't be tied up in other meetings." Each item was then assigned an owner, so that the takeaways would have someone accountable. For those two specific suggestions, I was able to get wireless installed on our floor and worked with the business sponsor to ensure that the business subject matter experts all had posted availability for the week. Having a discussion about what can be done better is a great idea, but it makes more sense to do this *during* the project, when something can be done, opposed to *after* the project, when the paperwork gets filed away as shelf ware. Visibility is provided around what is working well and actions are assigned immediately.

INFORMATION RADIATORS

Besides co-location, what became important is what is termed information radiators. What this means is displaying key metrics, goals, targets, team pictures, etc., provides for visual stimulation to remind the team what is important. In this particular project, we had many pictures of the team, the key goals for each week/month, and the progress toward them as I would update them daily, the main purpose for the project, and any special phrases or sayings that were inspirational that came from the team. Information radiators provide visibility for the team to reinforce what is important and have everyone see what the goals are.

The system consolidation project was no different than any other large-scale IT project where we had resource issues, demanding business customers, tight budget constraints, and fire drills, but providing visibility and allowing the business team to engage in the project daily and see the results helped to set and manage expectations. Once expectations are managed and visibility is provided into the team's progress and issues, the difficult conversations become easier to have and the bridge between the IT teams and business teams becomes easier to navigate.

3.4.3 Presenting and Sharing Information

Through listening, MBWA, and facilitation, a project manager can gain information, but there is also skill required in presenting that information to stakeholders in a way to achieve desired outcomes. The way that information is organized and the story it tells is a major contributor to how influential a message is. There are many aspects to a project manager's job where presenting information is important:

- Describing the project scope or approach. Early in projects there are many meetings where project managers will need to present the solution approach and scope of the project to other stakeholders. Ensuring that they understand the project goals will be critical to foster support for the initiative, get resources assigned, and have the project gain approval for funding.
- Describing a challenge and proposing recommendations. Projects always have challenges, risks, and issues that arise that require management attention. Clearly presenting the problem, impacts, and recommendations is essential to getting the decision needed from management. Unclear messages usually require additional work before a sponsor will make a decision, which can cause project delays.
- Communicating to the team. Presenting information in an informed and organized way demonstrates confidence to the team and can be used to motivate them. Keeping the team apprised of project issues and progress as well as any organizational changes is essential to having the team work together.

There are four key elements to presenting information:

1. Articulate the point. The information needs to be described in a way that the audience can understand. The relevant information should be the focus of the communication, and other information should be excluded or put in an addendum. If the information is being used to make a specific recommendation, then providing the why and not just the what is also important.
2. Show the end state. The communication should identify the information in the context of its target end state. This lets the audience know the progress that has been made, when the end state is, and how far is needed to go.
3. Show how the end state will be achieved. Explain the path and activities required to meet the end goal.

4. Describe the role of the audience. All of the right information may be in the communication, but if the audience cannot identify where they fit into the picture and what their role is, then often they won't identify with the message of the communication and take it to heart. For example, when a project manager raises an issue to management, it should be noted if this is something that management should be aware of or something that requires specific action.

Table 3.5 shows these four elements of presenting information in the context of three examples (a report, a presentation, and a meeting). While each of these is a different forum for presenting information, the core elements still apply.

There are several best practices that a project manager can use to present information effectively.

TABLE 3.5

Examples of Presenting Information

Attribute	Status Report	Presentation	Team Meeting
Key points (what)	• Status of project deliverables • Highlight risks and issues	• Main points of presentation (e.g., a decision is needed) • Why a decision is needed • Impact of options	• Information is being shared with the team (e.g., update on project work tracks)
End state (when)	• Target dates for deliverables • Dates for issue resolution	• The decision that needs to be made and the outcomes of that decision	• Team members' understanding of the project goals and current work
Path to end state (how)	• Activities required to complete deliverables • Actions to close issues or mitigate risks	• Information is presented to show how a particular recommendation will provide desired results	• Explanation of the information and how it relates to the overall project goals
Role of audience (who)	• Name resources required to complete deliverables • Call out items for management attention	• Identify the decision that needs to be made	• Explain to the team members their role with this information and how understanding it will help the project

3.4.3.1 Techniques and Skills

1. Technique—Communicating status. One of the most fundamental skills that a project manager can have is documenting and sharing the status of the project. Status reporting is more than just documenting every activity the team is working on; it should be considered the key communication vehicle to all project stakeholders. A good status report is clearly written and articulates what the team has accomplished, what needs to be accomplished, and any challenges with meeting project commitments.

   There are several items that should be thought of when documenting status:

   - Use a standard format. The reports should be consistent over time so that the readers become familiar with the layout and understand where they can find information. It also makes it easier to write the report each week. Most standard reports list the project name, key individuals, and the period of the report.
   - Keep it relevant. When the team is filling out their status reports, they should only articulate those items that are important to the progress of the project. Oftentimes resources see status reports as a way to justify their roles and show value by documenting as much as possible. This can clog up the communication with unnecessary noise, which masks the key points. The suggestion is for status reports to be in a bullet format with only a few bulleted items to promote the "promise of a conversation."
   - Color codes on status reports are an effective method of highlighting critical items and bringing attention to risks and issues.
   - Have an executive summary. Management doesn't always spend time reading through the status, so having an executive summary at the top of the status report or even in the e-mail text is an effective way to call out the key points.
   - Maintain status (and other information that is relevant to the project team) in a common place that the team is aware of so they can retrieve information easily as they need it. Making it difficult to find project documents will cause people to avoid looking for them, and they may miss out on important information required to perform their job.

2. Technique—Presenting information well. Presenting information is both a set of techniques and a skill because it combines the ability

to organize information properly with having effective communication skills to get the message across. There are some considerations and best practices for presenting information to different audiences:

- Tell a story. Creating slides or a report that has many bullets or doesn't flow can be confusing to the audience and not have the intended results. A presentation should clearly tell a story based on facts. For example, a story could be: "We had a problem on the project, it had these impacts based on specific facts, and we recommend a specific solution for these reasons." One good technique for presentations is using a sentence on the title part of the slide to describe the key point of that slide.

- Know the audience. Considering who the presentation will be given to should influence how the presentation is created. For example, some executives like the end results presented first, with the supporting data as backup, and some like the information to build up to the end results. Also, some managers like a lot of data to support findings and some like to see abstract diagrams.

- Use diagrams and visuals. Visuals are an effective way to highlight key messages. They also break up presentations that are all text, where key points can be missed because they were buried in paragraphs.

- Modify volume and pace. When presenting, a project manager should use his or her voice to accentuate key messages at points in time. This can also include pausing at particular moments so the audience can absorb the message being delivered.

- Anticipate questions. Preparing for the presentation should include considering what difficult questions can be asked. Using peers to review presentations is a good method to see how the information will be received and what questions might be asked.

- Focus on format. While the content of the presentation is the most important component, the format should also demonstrate high quality. Presentations with unaligned bullets, inconsistent fonts, and unorganized content appear sloppy, which may take away from the credibility of the content. A presentation should be seen as a reflection of the quality that a project manager expects from his or her team and from his or her own work.

- Pause and ask for feedback. Instead of presenting straight through the meeting, it is a good idea to stop after key points. This lets the information soak in and allows the presenter to gauge interest and audience reaction.

- Don't read the slides to people. The worst presenters are the ones who have all text in their slides and then just read it to the audience. Not only does it assume that the audience cannot read for themselves, but it is painful to participate in. Rather, the presenter should call out key points of the slide.
- Watch audience reactions. A project manager needs to be aware of the reactions of the audience and tailor his or her methods accordingly. If the audience is disengaged, a presenter might want to call on them to ask for their thoughts or speed up to the critical pages to capture their attention.
- When appropriate use humor. Humor is an effective way of keeping an audience engaged in the presentation. The humor needs to be appropriate for the audience and somewhat related to the topic of the presentation.

There are many methods that a project manager can use to improve upon presentation skills.

- Practice, practice, practice. There is never a limit to the amount of experience that someone can have with presenting. Therefore, a project manager should look for as many opportunities as possible to present information to an audience. This doesn't have to mean work and can include presenting at charity events, conferences, or local community forums. Getting comfortable presenting is fundamentally important to getting a point across because nervous presenters have a hard time staying focused on the message and can be distracting.
- Join an organization that focuses on presentation skills. Toastmasters is an example of a professional organization aimed at improving presentation skills by discussing techniques and practicing speaking in a safe environment.
- Watch others speak. While everyone's style is different, it is helpful to observer successful presenters to see how they deliver messages. Take notice of how they interact with the audience, get their points across, and pace themselves.
- Videotape a presentation. Watching oneself present is an effective way of seeing what the audience sees and having the ability to improve presentation skills. People are always amazed at what they see when they watch themselves present.

3. Technique—Sharing information. Given the complexity of projects and the many moving parts, the sharing of information within a project is essential. As part of their communication plan, project managers should have identified the different areas that require information and have also created a plan to keep them informed.

There are several best practices when sharing information with stakeholders:

- Communicate the why behind the what. This provides context for the information as opposed to just telling it to people.
- Create a common central location for information. The team should have a location and be aware of where they can go for the information.
- Encourage team members to share information with each other.
- Use part of the team meeting to share information, but make sure it is not just the project manager speaking.
- Share relevant information. The project manager should understand the recipient of the information and then share information appropriately based on his or her point of view and style. Some people like to hear all of the details, and other people just want to hear information when there is a problem.

Case Study: The Storyteller, the Wordsmith, and the Punch-Liner

Contributed by Kerry Wills

I was managing a large program for nearly two years, and over that time I learned the different styles of the stakeholders that I needed to communicate with. Specifically, there were three stakeholders who had very different styles of communication, and I needed to tailor my messages to them accordingly. For purposes of this case, I will refer to them as the storyteller, the wordsmith, and the punch-liner.

THE STORYTELLER

This was the executive sponsor of the program. He was very senior in the organization, and we had monthly steering committee meetings with him. His style of absorbing information was to have a story told, leading him to the conclusions. In these steering committee meetings I had a standard one-page status report with four quadrants: program budget, program highlights, key risks, and key issues. I also had a color code over each quadrant that called out the health of that item. Green meant everything was on track. Yellow meant there were some concerns and those items

were informational. Red meant there were risks with meeting project commitments that needed management action. This was a simple way to keep
the meeting focused on the big issues and also clarify which items needed
attention and which items were for informational purposes.

Beyond the status report there were also topical presentations. I remember one topic in particular where we were having problems with the data
in the system. We pulled together a presentation that outlined the story in
the following manner:

- Describe the problem. We described the area of the system and then
  highlighted the data problem in that context.
- Quantify the problem. We gave statistics on the number of policies
  that were having the data problem to get a sense of the magnitude of
  the issue. We made sure to outline the problem using facts.
- Give examples and show impacts. Using screen shots, we showed
  several examples of the data problem and then called out the impacts
  of those data problems.
- Give options. We listed several options for the data problems and
  gave the pros and cons of each with the associated cost and schedule implications.
- Make recommendations. After describing the options we gave recommendations from the team.

By telling the story in this manner, we led the executive through the issue,
gave a fact-based explanation of the impacts, and walked him through the
options with recommendations. Ultimately, he agreed with our recommendations and approved us to move forward with them. I feel that without
walking him through the story, we would have been caught up in cycles
of questions and fact gathering, which would have taken more time and
impacted project commitments.

THE WORDSMITH

The business sponsor on the project was a very detail-oriented person who
focused on specific words of messages. He read every word of every message and had very detailed questions about each of them. We learned
quickly to communicate with him via conversation as opposed to written
words because e-mails are hard to get key points across, and we tended to
get caught up on different topics.

To run meetings with the wordsmith we brought lots of data and facts.
We also brought in experts from the project team who could debate points
at the most detailed level. As the program manager, I was not well versed in
the minutia of the requirements, and it was very hard for me to have scope
discussions at this level. By having facts and people who could articulate
them in a manner the wordsmith understood, we learned how to effectively communicate to him and get the outcomes that we needed.

THE PUNCH-LINER

The IT sponsor on the program was the opposite of the storyteller. Instead of leading him up to the conclusions, he wanted to start with the "punch line" first. Anyone who presented to him with a story quickly learned that he would tear the pages out of the presentation and start with the last slide first.

The punch-liner was very particular about how he wanted information presented to him. You needed to start with the executive summary and conclusions first. Then follow with slides that had key messages to them. Each slide needed one message in the header (a title such as "problem statement" was not sufficient, it needed to be a sentence of the problem) and facts on the slide to back up that message. The slides also had to flow together so that someone could read the title messages of each slide and they told a story (but starting with the punch line first). Everything else then went into the appendix.

CONCLUSIONS

What I learned over the course of this program was that the same information could be presented in several different ways, depending on the audience. Some people want to start with the end, some people want to be walked through the story, and some people want to debate facts. It is important for the project manager to understand each audience type and then tailor the presentation and messages to them accordingly.

3.5 LEADING THE TEAM

Regardless of the organizational relationships of the project team, the project manager is the primary leader of the project. He or she is being held accountable by management to meet project commitments and is looked to for direction from the team members. The project manager can increase his or her rigor on projects, use a consultative approach to influence others, and communicate effectively, but his or her success is directly dependent on his or her ability to lead the project team members to meet their goals.

The biggest change needed for project managers in the new business landscape is that they must evolve from a project manager who manages the plan with direct control over resources to a project leader who has to influence and motivate the team through soft skills. Table 3.6 illustrates the differences in these two roles across several attributes.

For all of the reasons described in Chapter 2 of this book, the manager style described above is not effective in the new project world. Leading

TABLE 3.6

Project Manager vs. Project Leader

Attribute	Project Manager	Project Leader
Team relationship	• Has direct reports	• Has followers
View of role	• Team works for him or her	• He or she works for the team
Style	• Manages work	• Leads people
Decision	• Makes decisions	• Facilitates decisions
Directs	• Tells how and when	• Sells what and why
Power	• Uses authority	• Uses influence
Energy	• Control	• Passion
Wants	• Results	• Achievement
Concern	• Being right	• Doing what is right
Credit	• Takes	• Gives
Blame	• Gives	• Takes

projects today requires project managers to be able to motivate their team, empower them to be successful, and act as a champion for the team. As Figure 3.9 shows, these leadership skills focus primarily on the project team with support from the project leader. The project leader views the project organization as a relationship where the project leader works for the project team and not the other way around.

3.5.1 Motivating Team Members

In an environment where the project manager does not have direct control over the resources and has many part-time team members and non-employees, the ability to motivate them becomes crucial for success. Also,

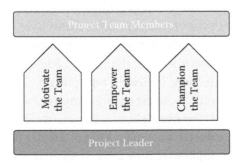

FIGURE 3.9

Project leadership elements.

projects today are often long in duration and people tend to lose motivation over the course of time. It is the project manager's responsibility to keep people engaged and focused throughout the course of the project.

Having a motivated team yields many benefits:

- Productivity is higher for people who are excited about their work, as they are willing to do more and stay later, if needed.
- Quality improves because there is an attention to detail and interest in the work being performed. Motivated people focus better and produce better results than unmotivated people.
- People who are motivated have less desire to look for other opportunities and leave the project. This will result in stability of the project team, which is important because having team members leave during projects can add cost and duration to the project to find and train replacements.
- Talented resources will want to join the team. People outside project teams hear about the teams that are excited, doing good work, and working well together and want to join them. There is no better recruiting engine for a project than its reputation.

There are some effective practices that a project manager can use to motivate the people on his or her team.

3.5.1.1 Techniques and Skills

1. Technique—Expect and recognize excellence. Foundational to motivating a project team is having clear goals and expectations of excellence for the team. By encouraging high but attainable goals, the project manager is demonstrating confidence in the team's ability to deliver the project and setting the stage for success. The project manager should work with the team to create a project vision statement that outlines these goals. The project manager should also have high standards for quality from all team members and ownership of the quality of their work (also known as quality at the source). Some examples include:
   - Reviewing all work before handing it off. The onus of quality needs to be on the worker producing the work and not on the recipient of it. For example, a developer should test the code and not produce it with an expectation of a tester finding the defects. Another example would be a business analyst confirming his or her requirements are sound before handing them off to a technical team member to design.

- Presentation of work. There is something to be said for the format and presentation of work. While it should be the content that matters, the format is sometimes viewed as a representation of the quality of someone's work and how much he or she cares about it. Don't underestimate how a messy presentation of work can trump the quality of the content.
- Encourage team members to set ambitious goals for quality. Rather than the project manager setting these goals, having the project team members create them enables more ownership of them.

Once the goals have been set, the project manager should look for opportunities to acknowledge and recognize excellence. Oftentimes project managers don't feel the need to recognize team members because there is a feeling that they are just doing their jobs. Team members who feel respected and valued will perform better on their tasks and are more likely to stay loyal to the project. There are many ways that a project manager can recognize people, without spending a lot of money:

- Send a message to the team, copied to management, highlighting key accomplishments and their results for customers. This demonstrates pride in and support for the project team members.
- Share successes in a team meeting.
- Write a handwritten note of gratitude.
- Hand out small tokens of appreciation, such as gift cards.
- Have a pot-luck lunch celebration.

Recognition should be considered part of the project management approach and communication approach of the project and done on a regular basis. Acknowledgment shouldn't be treated like an annual event or holiday.

There are a few cautions for recognition that need to be considered:

- Don't recognize everything. Like having lobster every night for dinner, recognition can be too much of a good thing and lose its sense of being special. Only key accomplishments and milestones should be acknowledged.
- Be sensitive to the behaviors that are being rewarded. Recognizing a team member who worked the weekend to fix his or her poor quality and ignoring the team member who met his or her deadlines while still working a forty-hour week may be rewarding the wrong actions. Team members who consistently do good work but do not get recognized may become de-motivated.

- Recognition should not be viewed as manipulation. Recognition needs to be seen as a genuine acknowledgment of success, as opposed to a way of "tricking" people into doing things.

2. Skill—Inspire the team. The project manager needs to inspire the team and a desire for accomplishments on a daily basis. Inspiring the team starts with the project manager showing enthusiasm and commitment to the project. Having a project manager who is not excited about the work makes it very hard for the team to be excited.

Once the project manager is committed and enthusiastic, he or she must focus on how to infuse this in the team. "Motivation always comes from within, not outside, a person. People are motivated in ways that will satisfy their internal needs, wants or concerns" (Lewis, 1998, page 34). Project managers need to understand these needs and relate to them so that people will feel inspired to work toward the project goals. Some examples of different motivators for project team members include:

- Working on a new challenge that has not been done before
- Working with new technologies and approaches (such as agile)
- Working with good people on a fun team
- Learning a new business area or function
- Having a sense of pride in improving an area of the company
- Working on a project that has a lot of visibility and recognition
- Having an opportunity for a stretch role or developing skill sets
- Being part of a high-performing team that has a specific team identity and reputation

A project manager needs to understand what motivates each person on the team so he or she can determine how to best inspire that person to achieve his or her highest productivity. Some considerations for doing so are highlighted below:

- Take a team assessment. There are assessments that an entire team can take that highlight motivators and personality styles for individuals. This can give the project manager some insight into the drivers of his or her team members. This can also be used as a team building activity, especially early on, when the project is just forming.
- Ask them. As described in prior sections in this book, the project manager should be building relationships with the team members as well as walking the floor interacting with them (MBWA). Building on these techniques, a project manager can ask team

members for their goals and to describe what excites them. Not only will this help the project manager determine the best way to motivate them, but it will strengthen their relationship because the project manager is demonstrating that he or she is listening and has empathy toward the team.

- Be observant of people's reactions and work habits. Sometimes the way a team member performs his or her job can be telling of his or her motivators. For example, if a team member does not interact much with other team members and spends his or her entire day at the computer, he or she may be motivated by the technical aspects of his or her work and not the social aspects. Other team members may be looking for acknowledgment of their work and are motivated by recognition.
- Explain to people how their contributions support project goals. It is hard for people to be motivated to work on something when they do not understand how it is impacting the greater cause.

3. Skill—Be honest and genuine. Beyond having high expectations for the team and inspiring people to do their work, the project manager must act in the same manner that he or she is asking from others As Albert Einstein said, "Example is not the main thing in influencing others. It is the only thing." There are many ways that a project manager can demonstrate high standards and integrity.

- Always be honest and genuine. People can tell very quickly if someone is not genuine and out for their best interests. This trust has to be established up front and then consistently demonstrated.
- Take ownership and accountability. The project manager needs to recognize that he or she is accountable for the project's success and its failures. Assigning blame is probably the worst way to ensure that the team will follow the project manager. People will hide problems, not share information, and be less motivated to work for someone who they perceive as blaming others.
- Demonstrating the ability to learn from mistakes. Showing the team that a project manager is human and makes mistakes can help the manager relate to the team. Taking these mistakes and learning from them is also a powerful form of leadership, which is also a good way to inspire people.
- Show trust of others. A project manager who empowers capable resources and demonstrates trust in them will have loyal followers.

- Be enthusiastic about each person's contributions. Encouraging opinions and ideas from team members and recognizing their importance shows people a genuine interest in what they have to offer. It will foster more collaboration and information sharing, which will improve morale and the quality of outcomes for the project.
- Clear hurdles. Helping to clear obstacles that team members have raised is a powerful way to show the commitment that a project manager has to the team. The result will be a commitment back to the project by the resources.
- Be consistent. Team members get frustrated with constantly changing expectations. Since stakeholders are usually the ones with the volatile requirements and expectations, the project manager needs to help corral these and maintain consistency for the team.
- Keep commitments. If a project manager makes a commitment to the team, then he or she needs to honor that commitment. This includes facilitating feedback and promising action. It is better not to ask for feedback than to ask for it and then not act on it because an expectation has been set with the team.

Case Study: Motivating Team Members for Success

Contributed by Chris Richards

BACKGROUND

As a program management consultant I had the opportunity to manage a large IT application re-platform project. The effort was multiyear, behind schedule, and massively over budget. When I joined the project, the team had already experienced multiple leadership changes, of which I was the third new program manager. With the previous leadership they had also experienced multiple attempts at defining the project strategy and direction. Each time these changes occurred the project fell further behind and the pressure to perform from senior management mounted. The result was extremely poor morale and a general sense of confusion on how to achieve success.

Being the proverbial "third man in the match," I set to the due diligence and quickly identified several daunting challenges. First, several of the projects were fixed items in that the scope was unable to be changed. For the business to realize the benefits and to continue to be competitive in the marketplace, it had to get off its old system and onto a new one. Staying where they were was a simple no-go. The budget was also a problem. Being significantly behind and with not much to show for it, senior management was hesitant to provide more dollars until a viable plan and strategy for success had been presented, accepted, and put into motion. The last significant challenge identified as a part of the diligence was the team. During the interview process I utilized the Ken Blanchard situational leadership model to assist in determining where the team lay. Out of this I quickly determined that most, if not all, fell into the category of high competence and low/variable commitment. In looking at their resumes, it was very apparent that they came with excellent pedigrees and experience. As a part of the interview process I asked them very specific questions regarding their experiences with the project: where they thought the issues lay, the challenges of the past, and what they thought they needed to be successful for the future. Past the technical and schedule challenges, much of the feedback focused on the strategy and the various leadership styles they had operated under.

THE PREDECESSORS

Their first leader had been exceptional by all accounts—exceptional at managing up. The PM spent the majority of his time hobnobbing with the leadership team and very little time setting the strategy and providing guidance and direction to the team. This became that individual's undoing. The team worked tirelessly toward nothing because of a lack of direction. Without direction or strategy, they soon ground to a halt. Subsequently and in time, the leadership team saw through the misleading status and replaced the lead.

The second PM had a much different leadership style than the first. While he did not manage up as much as the first PM, he took the lack of progress in the project as a call to arms. A self-labeled micromanager and technical specialist, he supervised and dictated every detail, including design and implementation. The PM's style quickly wore thin on the team. Suggestions for project improvements, especially when in conflict with the PM's, were often met with ire and disregard. The result was a poorly motivated team of highly talented people who eventually became unwilling to raise important issues for fear of reprisal. This was the undoing of PM 2. The technical direction chosen had several design flaws, and it was not long before issues started to arise. As those issues arose, the PM was quick to blame the team, technology, the organization, and the environment of the project failures. Normally, this strategy might have worked. This could have been true had the PM not made the repeated point that the change in direction and architecture was his call and not that of the team.

THE ROAD FORWARD

After completing the due diligence and my assessment, I made it a point to do two main things to motivate the team: The first was to recognize that I had a highly talented group of people on the team. Given that the project was behind schedule and budget, I sought their input into how and where to change the plan and architecture toward success. This did a couple of things. The plan then became the team's rather than that of an individual or that of the leadership. When the plan was complete and the team felt it was ready for prime time, I included them in the presentation to senior management. Each member was given a speaking part in the meeting. As a result, they were tied at the hip with the plan and felt vested in the solution. This carried through not only to how they viewed me as a leader but also to how they felt about the project. In the end, it became "our" project rather than "my" project. Thus, they worked extremely hard, ensuring success, as they all saw themselves as shareholders in the project.

The second and most important thing I did was to assign "I" to the problem and told the team directly that I would be their champion. When things went well, I gave them the lion's share of the praise, and when things went wrong (and occasionally they did), I'd stand up and take ownership and protect the team. While this seems simple in practice it's often the most overlooked and easy thing to sidestep when the heat gets turned up. After all, nobody likes being a bullet sponge for the steering committee to fire away at. In the end, it's important to remember at those moments that being a leader is more than just lip service. It means calling the shots, and occasionally receiving them. Leading from the front also had some large benefits. Over time and as I demonstrated my commitment, the team became fiercely loyal and hard working. Did they do it for my charming personality? While I'd love to think so, it definitely was not that. They did it because they were able to back somebody who was willing to sacrifice for the team and not ask of them what I was unwilling to do myself.

THE RESULTS

The result of the two basic motivational strategies above provided the greatest benefits out of all of the changes implemented to bring the project to a successful completion. This is not to say that it didn't have its challenges—it did. We delivered the project nearly a full year late and over budget. However, while over time and over budget, we were able to shave nearly a half year off the original replan, and subsequently saved hundreds of resource hours. The project is now several years past, and many of the team members have grown and gone on to new roles. As time has gone by, I still remain close to several due to the experiences and challenges we lived and shared together. At the end of the day the team still lives on.

3.5.2 Empower the Team

Once team members are motivated to be on the project and meet project commitments, the project manager should look for opportunities to empower the team. Empowerment is where a project manager distributes authority of portions of the project to other team members. Giving up control may be difficult for some people to do, but it is an effective method of increasing productivity and demonstrating leadership.

There are many benefits of empowering the team:

- Team members are much more motivated because they are contributing and "being allowed to shine." People will be more excited to do the work if they come up with it than if someone tells them what to do. Also, their confidence and enthusiasm to work for someone who empowers them is much higher than someone who tries to control them or tell them what to do.
- The overall outcomes of the project are better. Involving others, using their expertise, and letting them lead provides different perspectives that ultimately result in better project outcomes. Project managers need to recognize that sometimes the best decisions are not always made from management.
- Better focus for the project manager on critical items. When team members are empowered, progress is made without oversight of the project manager, so that his or her time can be spent on critical items such as proactive risk management, conflict resolution, or planning ahead for upcoming activities.
- Team members grow and learn new skills when put in stretch roles. This is a strong motivator for team members.

In order for team empowerment to achieve benefits, there are some conditions that need to be satisfied:

- Qualified team members. Project managers need to be aware of the strengths and interests of the project members so they can delegate work to the right people. Giving work to someone who isn't equipped to manage that work can be a risk to the project. If a resource doesn't have the experience, a project manager can recognize this as a stretch assignment and provide the resource with the support its needs to be successful.
- Team has resources required to complete work. Delegating work is only effective if the person that is being empowered is set up for success by having the resources he or she needs. It is the project manager's responsibility to ensure that the team has what they need to meet their goals.

- Understanding of goals and relationship of work. The team member who is being empowered needs to clearly understand the goals and context of the work that he or she is doing so he or she can be effective.
- Regular reporting of progress. As the person accountable for the overall project commitments, the project manager needs to be aware of the progress of the activities that have been delegated.

Beyond meeting the criteria listed above, empowerment is not the right technique for all resources. A project manager needs to recognize when a team member is capable of having work delegated to him or her. In their breakthrough work, Ken Blanchard, Paul Hershey, and Dewey Johnson (1997) created a model called situational leadership. This model suggests that managers must use different styles depending on the situation and the individual. There are two dimensions to their model around the approach of the leader to the resources: directive and supporting behavior. These styles directly relate to the two dimensions of characteristics of the followers: competency and commitment. There are four quadrants of leader styles in the model based on the follow characteristics.

- Telling/directing (high directive and low supportive)—This style is where the leader defines the roles and tasks of the follower and supervises him or her closely. Decisions are made by the leader and told to the follower. This model is best used for people who lack the competence but are enthusiastic and committed to the goals. These can include new employees.
- Selling/coaching (high directive and high supportive)—Leaders define the roles but seek ideas and suggestions from the follower. Decisions still remain with the leader but communication is more two-way. This is for people who have some competence but lack commitment and motivation. They need direction because they are relatively inexperienced and also need support to build their engagement.
- Participating/supporting (low directive and high supportive)—Leaders pass day-to-day decisions to the follower. The leader facilitates and takes part in the decisions, but the control is with the follower. This is for people who have the competence but lack motivation. They do not need direction because of their skills, but support is necessary to increase their commitment.

- Delegating (low directive and low supportive)—Leaders are still involved in decisions and problem solving, but control is with the follower. The follower decides how and when the leader will be involved. This is for people who have both commitment and confidence. They are capable of working independently with very little supervision.

Recognizing these different scenarios, a project manager should look to delegate work to the project team members who have both high competence and high commitment. These are motivated people who are experts in their areas, such as a technical lead, business analyst lead, or quality lead. The project manager can also look to delegate work to people with high competence and low commitment, but must recognize that those people will require more support. Delegating work to people with low competency (and especially those with low commitment) can be a risk to the project because they won't have the background or support structure to be successful.

3.5.2.1 Techniques and Skills

Empowerment is more than just putting the name of a team member next to a set of deliverables on the project plan. There are some techniques that a project manager can use to effectively empower the team.

1. Technique—Delegate the work. Delegating project work means making individual team members responsible for a portion of the project and also giving them authority over the deliverables and activities. The project manager is still accountable for the overall project, but he or she is assigning deliverables or work tracks to team members and making them the leaders of that work.

    There are several best practices when delegating work to team members that should be considered:
    - Delegate specific chunks of work as opposed to pieces. Team members should be assigned whole pieces of work. Assigning partial work to several people results in confusion over responsibilities and the potential for missed work because each person thought another person was working on it.
    - Delegate the good stuff. Don't just delegate the boring administrative work; delegate some of the fun work also. This can

include important components of work and visible meetings with management.

- Recognize what work cannot be delegated. Not all project work should be delegated to team members, such as personal or confidential activities.
- Define the outcome but not the means. Part of empowering the team is to let them come up with the solutions, so a project manager should delegate the deliverables or outcomes but then let the lead determine the best approach.
- Confirm the limits of authority. The project manager needs to make the empowered people aware of the scope of their authority with regards to the delegated work. For example, a lead may be accountable for the technical design of the solution but not the build and implementation of it.
- Assign stretch roles to leads. A project manager should delegate slightly more than he or she thinks the person is capable of handling. The project manager should make sure, however, that the person it set up to succeed with the appropriate resources and support structures available to him or her.
- Never take back the work. If the delegated lead is not performing the activity to expectations or fast enough, the project manager should look for ways to coach him or her or provide support to be successful. The work should not be taken back from the individual unless there is a significant performance problem. This will send the wrong message to the team and be seen as punitive as opposed to empowering.
- Give the credit. The project manager needs to make sure that the leads of the work get the appropriate recognition for their efforts. People will become resentful if they think that the project manager is taking credit for the work that they have done. The project manager should provide credit all of the time, which in turn also helps his or her reputation among both team members and leaders.

2. Technique—Solicit input from the team. Empowerment doesn't have to be delegating specific work to team members. It can also be the way that a project manager uses the team members to plan for and run the project. Recognizing that in most cases he or she is not an expert in the business or in the technologies being used, the project manager should encourage the sharing of expertise from his or her team members. Beyond getting a better and more realistic plan, the

result of involving team members is buy-in to the project commitments and plan (as described in Section 3.2.3.)

There are several examples in a project where a project manager can empower the team to provide input, including:

- Planning. As described in Section 3.2, it is critical to involve resources in the planning of the work because they are the experts in their respective fields and understand the nuances that need to be planned for.
- Designing the solution. Because of the complexities required to design solutions, it is important to involve the right people. For example, involving the people who need to maintain a system during the design of it could provide a different perspective into how the system is architected.
- Crisis situations. The project manager should solicit input and recommendations from the team during crisis situations. The crisis is usually a function of a specific set of events, which the team members can decompose and provide solutions to. In this case a project manager is empowering the team to resolve the situation. Remember that the project manager should be the facilitator of solutions and not necessarily the problem solver for every crisis. That takes away the ownership of the solutions.

3. Technique—Encourage open communication, collaboration, and trust. Fundamental to the use of empowerment is open communication and collaboration on a project. Because there are many moving parts with several leads that have authority, communication is imperative to understand the status of work so that it can be planned for and managed effectively. Collaboration is also critical because most work tracks are reliant on other work tracks or stakeholders. Therefore, leads need to be able to work with other leads to meet their common goals.

A project manager needs to establish an environment where team members are comfortable expressing their comments and feel supported to experiment with new concepts. Team members should be encouraged to contribute in brainstorming sessions and commended for providing input. This open environment will generate new ideas and establish a more team-oriented culture on the project.

Some ways that a project manager can encourage an environment of open communications and collaboration include:

- Having team events. Creating team activities where different stakeholders and members from the teams can get together is an effective way of building rapport and relationships that the project manager can leverage during the project. This is especially important early in a project, when people do not know each other very well.

- Rewarding collaboration. Project managers need to recognize and reward examples of collaboration across the team. These can be acknowledged at team events or by a message to the managers of the resources.
- Demonstrating the value of feedback. Project managers should constantly demonstrate appreciation for receiving feedback and never punish someone for stating his or her opinions. If people think they will be punished, then they will not participate in communications and may have important information or insights that do not get shared.
- Recognizing when people are not participating or are building walls. A project manager needs to be observant of his or her team to see who is not communicating or collaborating well and seek to understand the cause.

Case Study: Delegating for Better Outcomes

Contributed by Kerry Wills

After successfully managing several projects early in my career, I was given the opportunity to plan for and run a multi-million-dollar program. On the projects that I had run in the past I had gotten deep into the details and understood all of the business requirements and technical aspects because they were smaller in size. Since this program was the largest that I had run, I quickly realized that there was no way that I could stay on top of all of its pieces (and still have a life outside of work).

I set up a program structure that delegated the work to leads that were accountable for the different components of the program.

- Project managers who were accountable for the execution of their pieces of the program
- A business engineering lead who was accountable for all of the business components across the program, such as requirements, testing, training, and business rollout
- A technical engineering lead who was accountable for all of the technical aspects across the program, including design, build, architecture, and infrastructure

At first, it was hard for me to give up this control, having been successful in my career as a result of being in the details. I had to trust the leads and let them own their own pieces, which was hard to do. What I quickly came to realize were the benefits of delegating the work:

- As a team we were more productive because there were many people working on critical aspects of the program at the same time. I wasn't being a bottleneck for work or decisions, because the work was spread across the leads.
- Having the leads accountable for their pieces allowed me to free up time for forward-looking planning or help them resolve issues.
- We had better solutions because there was good dialogue between the leads, which I could then facilitate.

I learned a lot from my experiment with delegation and continue to be conscious of this technique as I run other work today. That being said, I do still like being in the details, so I try to balance the delegation with an understanding of the work being done.

3.5.3 Be a Champion for the Team

Once the team is motivated to work on the project and empowered to manage portions of it, the project manager needs to become a champion for the team. This means accepting and promoting the recommendations from the team and supporting them during critical situations. It is not enough to empower the team to own work if they do not feel like they will be supported by management.

Some characteristics of a project champion include:

- Believer in the cause. Consistently demonstrating confidence and commitment to all project commitments. This means that a project manager's actions need to always match his or her words.
- Advocacy for the team. This means supporting the project team with their recommendations and acknowledging their issues and risks. A project champion is vocal about his or her support and confidence in the team. Project managers who disparage their teams to others will have a very hard time getting people to want to work for them or follow them to meet project goals.
- Removing obstacles. As the team raises challenges or issues, the project champion should act to resolve them quickly so that the team can continue working toward project goals. Not only does this help the project move forward, but it is a great demonstration of commitment to the team members and results in a reciprocal loyalty.

Demonstrating rapid resolution issues will give people confidence in the project manager, and they will be more likely to raise other challenges early, before they become bigger problems.

A project manager needs to recognize himself or herself as a champion for the project team and act accordingly. This can be done by using the following techniques.

3.5.3.1 Techniques and Skills

1. Technique—Support the team. There are many stakeholders to satisfy, but the project manager must recognize that having the team's support and dedication is the only way to meet project commitments. To gain their support and loyalty, the project manager must support them as well. There are many situations in which the project manager can show support for the team:
   - During planning when the team gives estimates for the work. The project manager needs to plan based on the activities that the team determines, and not create the plan on behalf of the team. This will result in a lack of commitment to project goals because the team members were not part of defining the work. Supporting the team in this case may require the project manager to push back on dates if the team does not feel like they are feasible given the defined scope.
   - When challenges are presented to the project manager. One of the quickest ways for a team to lose confidence in the project manager is for issues or risks to be escalated and not acted on. A project manager needs to acknowledge the items raised and then resolve them quickly.
   - During conflicts with stakeholders or other areas. Project managers need to show support for their teams in times of conflict. Resolving conflicts on behalf of team members will build loyalty and trust for the project manager.

   When supporting the team, the project manager should consider some of the following techniques:
   - Have the courage to push back on management. A classic scenario on projects is when the team provides an estimate that management thinks is too high. Usually what happens is that management expects the estimate to be reduced, but not the scope of the project. The project manager needs to demonstrate confidence in the team's

estimate and look to negotiate a reduction in scope or schedule. This is a difficult situation, but an important one for the project manager to build trust from the team. If the project manager is viewed as always "caving in," then there will be no reciprocity of loyalty and the project will risk not meeting its commitments.

- Never use *I* or *you*, but rather *we*. When communicating on behalf of the project, the project manager should always speak on behalf of and as part of the team (e.g., "we worked on …"). In critical situations, using the word *you* when speaking to the team takes the project manager out of the team (e.g., "you need to work harder"). Also, when speaking to groups about the project, the project manager shouldn't talk about himself of herself (e.g., "I will meet the dates by …"). Either situation loses credibility with the project team and can result in reduced loyalty and trust.

- Recognize when the team says there is a problem. There are always challenges that arise during projects, but it is important that the project manager recognize them when they are communicated and demonstrate that he or she will act on them. A project manager who is viewed as dismissive of issues will not get them raised in a timely manner and will always be surprised by them when he or she does become aware.

- Communication is important. To support the team properly, the project manager must communicate when there are problems and how they will be addressed. This demonstrates to the project team that the project manager acknowledges their problems. The project manager should also be sure to communicate with the team on a regular basis, to let them know any relevant information.

2. Technique—Remove obstacles. To be a champion, the project manager needs to support the team not only in words but also in actions. This means removing any barriers to the project that get escalated by the project team. There are several common project situations that a project manager must recognize and take action on:

- When decisions need to be made. This is one of the most common pitfalls of a project—when decisions pile up and work slows down as a result. Because minor decisions may not be viewed as critical issues, they sometimes get overlooked but can have impacts on project commitments. A project manager needs to stay diligent in decisions and ensure that they get made.

- When third-party vendors or stakeholders are holding up work. Sometimes projects have dependencies on other areas that are not meeting their commitments. The project manager needs to resolve those situations quickly so that the project can continue to work toward its goals.
- When issues get raised. It is important to act on issues and resolve them early so that they do not have an impact on project commitments.
- Resource dynamics. The project manager needs to be observant of resource productivity and interactions. Having the right team members is all about the fit of the resource on the project. Sometimes resources need to be removed or added to the team to improve the productivity of the team.

By recognizing and then taking action to remove obstacles, a project manager keeps the team running toward their commitments and goals. This also results in a team that is loyal, enthusiastic, and more willing to raise other issues, because they know that they will have action taken on their behalf.

Case Study: Championing the Team to the Right Outcomes

Contributed by Kerry Wills

I was the program manager for a multi-million-dollar multiyear program that was aggregating the company's policies to understand the overall risk exposure. This program had been running for two years when I was asked to perform an audit of it because of some perceived challenges by senior management. As a result of the audit I had confirmed these challenges and proposed several recommendations to remediate them. Not only did senior management want to implement the recommendations, but they made me take over the program as the lead.

As a result of the audit it was clear that there were several major obstacles that needed to be cleared:

- Scope needed to be locked down. Two projects in the program were in the build phase, but requirements were not consolidated into one place, nor were they officially signed off on by the business sponsors. This led to many changes in scope, which were impacting the project commitments.
- Decisions needed to be made. During the audit interviews, several team members noted that they had decisions that were outstanding for weeks that were impacting their ability to complete activities.

- The project schedule and budget were not managed tightly. This made it hard to understand the impacts of the scope changes and open action items on the project commitments.
- The stakeholders were challenging. The key stakeholders had a disdain for managing scope and wanted what they wanted when they wanted it. Being told no was hardly an option regardless of what was documented.
- Team morale was low because the stakeholders kept pushing back on scope (and changing it), work was not being agreed to by other organizations, decisions were not being made, and roles were not clear.

When I took over the program I realized that I had a lot of work to do: restructuring the program, getting agreement on scope, making decisions, and improving the morale of the team. To do these, I recognized that I needed to involve and champion the team as much as possible or I would not be successful. This was especially important because I was joining the team late and needed to gain credibility quickly. Described below are the techniques that I used to solve the problems and still be a champion for the team.

SCOPE

Since the program had several projects in the build phase without signed-off requirements, the volatility of scope was high. This was called out in the audit, which was then passed on to the project sponsors, who did not take well to that message. In my first meeting with them, one of them pulled out a piece of paper with a few sentences on it and literally threw it at me across the table and said, "I don't know what you mean. The scope is right here!" I calmly picked it up, read it, and then looked at him and said, "When I read this it essentially says that you want a house. It doesn't say how many doors, electrical outlets, appliances, or light switches you want. We need more detailed requirements."

We then spent several (painful) weeks debating over specific words and scope statements until we had a consolidated list of what was in the scope for the program. Even then the key stakeholder refused to sign off on the document, for some fear that he would be held to every word in the document (he actually forbid us from using the words "change control" on the project, so we just referred to the list as "things you asked for that we did not estimate for in the plan, schedule, or budget"). In the end I told him that he did not have to sign the document, but I wanted to make sure that he knew what would be delivered at the end of the project so he could not say that he wasn't aware.

While these working sessions and scope discussions were incredibly hard, it was important to lock this down for the sake of the team. They could not do their jobs if the scope was nebulous, being challenged, or constantly changing.

DECISIONS

As I was locking down the scope, I also sat with each of the team leads across the program and asked them to tell me what work was outstanding and what decisions needed to be made. When I was done I had compiled a list of about thirty open decisions that were preventing people from completing their assignments. These included everything from decisions on technological solutions to resources that they needed to get assigned to the team. Within one month I had set up working sessions to determine the options and had made decisions on all of the items. While I am sure that not all decisions were optimal, at least they were made so that people could move forward. This demonstrated commitment to the team and support for their desire to meet their project goals.

PLAN

I also worked to lock down an achievable project plan by having many working sessions with the team leads to identify the remaining activities. This was important because there was not a very detailed plan that the team was aware of, let alone participated in the creation of. Within a few weeks we had detailed plans for each of the projects, and we also had an integrated view of the overall program. These plans then became handouts that team members posted on their work cubes.

STAKEHOLDER MANAGEMENT

Lastly, I needed to shield the team from some of the difficulties presented by some of the business stakeholders. I spent many meetings fielding the concerns of the stakeholders and preparing for ways to address them. This became a goal of mine so that the team could stay focused on their work and not on defending it in meetings. I found that using facts and having a coalition of other stakeholders at these meetings was successful at managing the expectations of the other leaders.

Within several months, the program had clarity of its structure, plan, and scope with very few open items. This allowed the team to focus on meeting the objectives of the plan, which resulted in their productivity and morale increasing.

There was one last challenge to overcome, which came a few months before the completion of the project. When we were testing the aggregated data, the team noted that while the technical integrations with other systems worked, the data themselves were suspect. Because the program was intended to focus on our risk exposure, having accurate data was critical. The team wanted to extend the project by two months to fully analyze and fix the data problems (which were from systems not part of the project directly). The project could have still met its date because the technology and integration were working to specifications, but the team believed that the integrity of the data was more important than the schedule commitment. This is where I made the decision to champion the team as opposed to focus on the project goal of meeting the schedule. As a project manager who is measured on delivering to schedule, this was a difficult decision to make, but it was the right one.

I had the team perform some analysis and gather facts and took their recommendation to the senior vice president and sponsor of the program. Because we used facts to demonstrate the impact of the bad data and came to him several months before the end of the project, he was open to the recommendation of extending the timeline.

As a result of listening to the team's concerns about scope, decisions, and data quality, and then being a champion for them by closing open issues, managing difficult customers, and extending the timeline, we completed the project with a high confidence in the results and pride in our work. This will allow the company to make better business decisions.

3.5.4 Handling Conflicts and Difficult People

There are always conflicts on projects that arise that have to get resolved. These result from people having different personalities, agendas, backgrounds, values, work styles, and convictions on how to accomplish work activities. Work conflicts, if not managed properly, can lead to low morale, decreased productivity, and even missed project goals and commitments. Some examples of common conflicts that can occur on a project include:

- Interpersonal conflicts can arise between project team members. When people work together closely, and especially under the stress of tight project deadlines, they sometimes get into arguments.
- Different interpretations of scope. Even though scope is well documented on projects (see Section 3.1.1), there is sometimes a conflict over what is supposed to be in the scope. This is the classic change management problem, where a project manager says that something is a change because it wasn't planned for or estimated, and a business customer says it is not a change because "that's what they meant and said" when they gave the original set of requirements.
- Inevitably on every project there is a difficult person to work with who is aggressive, confrontational, and sometimes mean. Every interaction with him or her seems to be a conflict. Sometimes these people are in positions of power and influence over the project (which is probably why they think it is acceptable).

- Since resources being used on projects are shared and sometimes scarce, there may be conflicts over getting resources when they are needed.
- Projects also have many stakeholders and interaction points. Late in projects, when something isn't working properly, there may be conflicts around why the solution is not working as expected and how to resolve it.

Whether the project manager is facilitating the resolution of a conflict or is involved in the conflict, he or she should focus on a few techniques to try to get to an agreeable solution.

3.5.4.1 Techniques and Skills

1. Technique—Address the conflict. Conflicts on projects are inevitable, so a project manager should expect them to occur. Sometimes people want to avoid conflicts, but in doing so they may be allowing a difficult situation to continue, which may have impacts on the success of the project. For example, there may be a sponsor who is constantly adding scope, telling people "just to suck it up," and acting aggressive when they are pushed back on. The result of avoiding a contentious situation with that sponsor will be additional scope that wasn't planned for and will have a material impact on the project costs and schedule.

   A project manager should consider the reasons why he or she might dislike conflicts and address them. Then the project manager should recognize the impacts of allowing those situations to occur.

2. Skill—Maintain composure. After accepting the conflict, the first step in managing it is to not immediately overreact. In the situation where the project manager is facilitating the conflict resolution, he or she needs to stay level headed, be perceived as neutral, and not become part of the conflict. In the situation where the project manager is in the conflict, he or she needs to stay calm so that a resolution can be found quickly. This is much easier said than done, but it ties back to the self-management principles described in Section 3.3. It is important to recognize that keeping relationships with people is important for long-term success, and not to give in to short-term emotions (i.e., not "burning bridges").

   If the project manager is involved in the conflict, then he or she needs to be conscious of his or her reactions and possibly step away or take a break before looking to resolve the issue. This may allow him or her to calm down, focus on gathering the right information, and prepare to have a sensible, fact-based conversation.

3. Technique—Pay attention to the messages to understand the conflict. It is important to pay attention and seek to understand the messages and perspectives that are being presented by the people involved in the conflict. By listening carefully, a project manager can understand why the person is adopting his or her position and what his or her key points are. To solve a problem effectively, a person has to understand where the other person is coming from before defending his or her own position. This requires the difficult skill of listening first, before talking or defending positions. A good technique to demonstrate listening and comprehension is to repeat back and summarize what the other person has said.

   Sometimes there are also underlying problems that don't get explicitly stated, so it is important to try to get to the root of the problem. If there are hints of underlying issues, the project manager should ask clarifying questions, for example, "It seems like something else is bothering you. Would you like to talk about it?" This may invite the other person to present additional information or insights.

   Another good technique for getting to the important messages is to acknowledge areas of agreement first, before moving into topics of disagreement. This starts the conversation with a common set of agreed topics so that the discussion can be facilitated around a specific target of topics.

4. Technique—Focus on the facts. Once people are calm and understand the positions involved in the conflict, the next focus should be on gathering the appropriate information. Instrumental to resolving a conflict is to center on the facts and not to make it personal with the people in the conflict. The project manager should never be seen as casting blame, which is why using facts de-personalizes the situation. Table 3.7 shows some examples of facts that can be gathered for common project scenarios.

   As shown in the examples above, conflicts that arise over work artifacts can be managed by having proper project documentation. This underscores the need for the execution rigor that is described in Section 3.2. It is very hard to have a debate over what scope is included in the project estimates late in the game when the scope documentation is loose and was not signed off on.

TABLE 3.7

Examples of Relevant Facts

Conflict Type	Facts
Team member interpersonal conflict	• Examples of what each person said (difficult because there are always interpretations—best to have third-party examples) • Examples of behaviors observed by others
Debate over scope	• Documented scope deliverables • Signed-off requirement deliverables • Meeting minutes
Resource not available when needed	• E-mails or other documents outlining commitments for resources • Plans to show impact of not obtaining resources on time
Technical problem that can impact the project	• Technical specifications • Test case results

When the conflicts are with difficult stakeholders or between team members, having facts is also important. It really is the only way to manage difficult people without getting into personal attacks and being "pulled down into the mud."

5. Technique—Consider a third-party mediator. Sometimes conflicts cannot be resolved with existing people. A project manager should be open to the idea that a third-party negotiator can be used to help resolve the situation. These people can be seen as neutral parties who will hear both sides and provide an independent perspective on the conflict.

6. Technique—Be flexible with the approach. Every conflict is different, and a project manager needs to recognize his or her approach to handling conflicts and be sensitive to the particulars of the situation. For example, the approach used to manage a scope interpretation may be to present facts and documents. However, a conflict between two coworkers related to their amount of authority on a project may require involvement from human resources and management.

To be flexible, a project manager needs to start with understanding his or her style of managing conflicts. There are a few ways to accomplish this:

- Ask others for feedback after a conflict to understand their perspectives on how successful the approach was and how they felt.

- Take a conflict-style assessment to get an outside perspective on conflict style and the appropriateness of that style for different situations.
- Reflect on prior conflicts and what could have been done differently given that particular situation.

Case Study: Good Worker but Bad Attitude

Contributed by Kerry Wills

I was working as the program manager for a large program in a Fortune 500 company. I have found that on almost every large program that I have worked on there is at least one difficult person on the team, and this program certainly had one. This individual was a contractor who had been on the team for a few years. She was very good at her work, but her interactions with the team were counterproductive for the other members on the project.

Some examples of her interaction style included:

- Always having to be right. This individual was clearly a perfectionist, and in every conversation she had to debate each point, no matter how insignificant it may be to the conversation, to make sure that it was "right."
- Could not deal with ambiguity. Any time there was an unclear request or lack of information she became uncomfortable and aggressive.
- Talked about other people. This individual was notorious for talking about people "behind their backs" and disparaging them to other people. She believed that she could perform any role on the project better than the people in those roles. Of course, this information got back to those team members.
- Dominated meetings. She had to interject her opinions in every meeting and take it over for her own agenda.
- Was always negative. When this person did contribute and speak, it was usually negative about the work, the project, the organization, or the people.

There were several impacts of her interactions on the team. Project team members did not want to work with her because they felt like she was condescending and would talk about them behind their backs. They also spent a significant amount of time in my office regarding this individual's behavior, as well as with each other, discussing the tirade of the day. This caused the team to be disjointed and focused on the wrong things. It amazed me that, as a contractor where we were her customers, this person would interact with the team in this manner. The challenge was that she did good work and the business liked her, so the behavior was tolerated.

I tried several techniques to manage her behavior and improve her relationships with the other team members.

- Relating to her. I tried discussing things that were important to this person, such as her background, interests, and even children (we both had family members with similar illnesses). While she was cordial to me during those interactions, it did not change the behavior, and at times our discussions did not feel genuine.
- Catering to her ego and experience. Knowing that this person was proud of her knowledge and skills, I went to her several times for advice, demonstrations, or information. I tried to use those as opportunities to acknowledge her experience and knowledge.
- Maintaining my composure. While many of the team members would fall into her trap and get into heated debates, I tried to take the "high road" and not allow myself to do the same. If this person was taking over meetings or taking the topic off course, I tried to calmly bring the meeting back to the topic.
- Discuss the facts. Knowing that this person was detail oriented, I modified my interactions to be focused on specific facts. However, because I was not an expert in the business processes or detailed requirements, we usually wound up discussing information at two different levels.

Through the course of the program I tried several techniques to manage this difficult person, but none of them seemed to work. At the time I did not confront her directly because of her relationship with the business sponsors, and I did not feel like I had the authority to do so. In hindsight I probably should have tried this technique as a last resort, because my inaction caused the team to continue to suffer.

In the end I wound up rolling this person off the program at a logical juncture by not extending her contract. While this did stop the pain for the project team, it was later than it probably should have been. I recognized too late how toxic her behavior was to the team and their morale and productivity.

4

Summary

4.1 TYING IT ALL TOGETHER

The previous chapters described the evolution of the project landscape and the subsequent skills required to be a successful project manager in the new world. Figure 4.1 summarizes the main steps in this evolution.

1. The business landscape has been changing recently due to several factors in the marketplace (Chapter 1).
2. As a result of the changing business landscape, there are new trends for delivering technology projects (Chapter 2).
3. These trends have impacts on projects that need to be considered when planning and managing them (Chapter 2).
4. To successfully manage a project in the new business environment, the project manager's skills need to change (Chapter 3).

To thrive in the new project environment, the project manager must focus on several different techniques and dimensions (as described throughout Chapter 3). There is not a "silver bullet" that a project manager needs to use to ensure that his or her project will meet all of its commitments. Rather, it is a combination of constant diligence (project management) and consultative skills (project leadership), and using them both effectively in the appropriate situations. Using one set of skills without the other will not work. Table 4.1 gives examples of the impact of only using one set of techniques on a project.

Both leadership and management skills are critical for project success. Chapter 3 described these techniques and skills in detail and suggested ways for how a project manager can use and strengthen them. Across these techniques and skills there are several consistent themes to highlight and summarize.

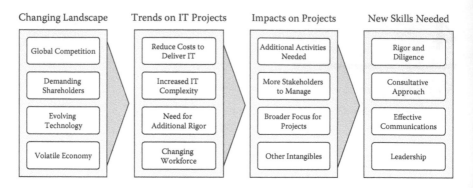

FIGURE 4.1
Summary of impacts and skills needed.

4.1.1 Planning Is an Investment

Because of the increased complexity in technologies, organizations, and business processes, it is critical to spend the appropriate time up front on projects. Planning has to be seen as an investment on behalf of the project's ability to confidently meet its commitments. An old proverb says, "Failing to plan is planning to fail." This is true now more than ever, given all of the considerations that projects must account for today.

A simple analogy can be driving to work in the morning. The goal is to make it to work in time for the first meeting, using the roads laid out in the plan. A person can get up in the morning, get in his or her car, and head out to work. Without planning, there can be several challenges that arise that will have an impact on the goal:

- There may be construction or an accident, causing delays, and by the time it is recognized, all of the exit ramps have been passed. This will result in missing the schedule goal.
- There may have been a snowstorm, with one foot of snow on the ground. There is now a change to scope since there is the added activity of shoveling the driveway and cleaning off the car. The schedule can also be impacted because of the slowdown in pace on the roads and possible road closures.
- There may be potholes in the road that aren't seen until they have been driven over, which may lead to a budget variance to buy new axles.

Instead of just getting on the road, there are several planning activities that could avoid the pitfalls listed above. Spending time watching the news

TABLE 4.1

Scenarios for Management and Leadership on Projects

Project Scenario	Description	Possible Results
Management without leadership	• Strong management of the plan and project deliverables • Rapid decisions • Lack of relationships with stakeholders • Lack of inspiration and empowerment for the team	• Possible turnover of team and low morale, which impacts project quality and commitments • Information is not obtained on a timely basis, resulting in more significant impacts of risks and issues • Team members not committed to project goals because they don't feel like they own the work or were involved in it
Leadership without management	• Good relationship with team members and stakeholders • Good communications with stakeholders • Plan not well organized • Issues and risks not followed up on diligently	• Decisions may not be made in a timely manner, causing delays in the project • Lack of visibility of the plan and progress • Delays in issue closure, which may impact the project
Leadership and management	• Strong management of the plan and project deliverables • Rapid decisions • Good relationship with team members and stakeholders • Good communications with stakeholders	• Motivated team • Information obtained quickly • Challenges resolved quickly • Progress of plan understood

in the morning would reveal any weather, traffic, or construction issues. Then the plan can be changed for a different route or to leave the house earlier to ensure that the goals are still met. Also, looking ahead in the road while driving will reveal any upcoming challenges, such as potholes or accidents, so that they can be avoided.

As described throughout Chapter 3, there are many important activities to account for early in the project, including:

- Project planning—Determining and documenting the project management approach, which includes planning for the operational components, organization structure, and use of tools and processes.
- Activity planning—Making sure that all activities are planned for, stakeholders are involved in the planning, and considerations such as rework, reviews, and methodologies are accounted for.
- Resource planning—Spending time on understanding resource needs, critical skills, and planning for backups as necessary.
- Communication planning—Determining a communications approach based on the audience needs.
- Metric planning—Defining what metrics will be used to monitor the progress of the project and how they will be communicated.
- Relationships building—Building relationships early so that they can be utilized throughout the project life cycle.
- Building influence and trust from the project team members—Starting off the project with a good perception from the team.

4.1.2 Constant Diligence

A project manager needs to remain diligent throughout the project. Good planning without diligent execution is time wasted. For example, spending a lot of time on a great project estimate but then not managing change controls well will invalidate the accuracy of the estimate. There are many areas that a project manager needs to stay on top of:

- Making decisions in a timely manner. Decisions can hold up project schedules if they are outstanding for a long period, and can also have rework if not made properly. A project manager needs to be aware of what decisions need to be made, use facts to facilitate that they get made, and document them for future reference.
- Acting on issues and risks. Recognizing issues and risks and acting on them quickly will allow the team to remain productive and focused.
- Continuing to gather and present information to stakeholders to keep them informed of progress and key challenges and risks.
- Managing the project deliverables. The project manager needs to understand the state of the project activities, resources, and financials at all times to understand progress and be able to communicate to all stakeholders effectively.

- Looking at metrics. Metrics will help the project manager to gauge the project health at all times and get an idea of areas to spend more time on.

A diligent project manager can manage all of the activities listed above to help the project continue progressing toward its goals. It is crucial not to fall behind on these items, because then the project quickly moves into a state of "chasing fires," being reactive to situations, and having items start to pile up and become unmanageable. The creation of a project management office can help with the operational diligence, which will keep the project manager focused on removing obstacles and supporting the team.

4.1.3 Making Time for the Right Things

Project managers must make sure that they prioritize their time to focus on high-value activities that will help them and their teams be successful. Chapter 3 outlined many techniques for being an effective project manager, but they all require being proactive and spending time on them. Some of the important activities where a project manager needs to spend time include:

- Looking ahead at the project plan to identify upcoming activities and plan accordingly for them
- Management by walking around (MBWA) to obtain critical project information and build rapport with team members
- Building and fostering relationships with team members and stakeholders
- Communicating project information to stakeholders
- Recognizing and celebrating successes
- Being available at his or her desk for real-time conversations and walk-ins from project team members
- Preparing for meetings by gathering information, soliciting input, and considering the audience
- Looking at informative metrics to understand the progress of the project and key risk areas
- Proactively considering risks to the project and the proper mitigations

There is an inverse relationship between the workload/meetings that a project manager has and his or her ability to focus on the proactive activities: the more time a project manager can free up, the more time he or she can spend on being proactive. What happens is that project managers can sometimes lose the ability to be proactive and only focus on the issues at

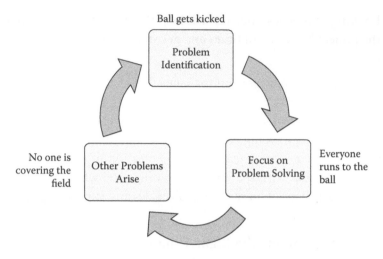

Ball gets kicked

Problem Identification

Everyone runs to the ball

Focus on Problem Solving

Other Problems Arise

No one is covering the field

FIGURE 4.2
Cycle of reaction in a soccer metaphor.

hand, which results in quickly falling behind in their ability to manage all of the project activities.

This spiral can be compared to watching children play soccer, where project teams are always chasing down the most recent problem, like children chasing down a soccer ball. It becomes a perpetual loop, diagrammed in Figure 4.2.

1. Problem identification. A problem gets identified on the team, which can be viewed as a soccer ball being kicked.
2. Focus on problem solving. This problem usually involves the entire team, or a large part of it, to solve, so everyone runs to where the ball is on the field.
3. Other problems arise. Because the team is focused on the problems at hand, they are not working on other aspects of the project, resulting in those areas having problems later. This can be viewed as not covering the field with players, but rather everyone running toward the ball.

In this cycle, the team is always behind the ball chasing it wherever it gets kicked. The result is the same for the project as it is in the children's game: a long time goes by without many goals being made. This is usually accompanied by lots of yelling from the sidelines by the coach (project manager). Once in this loop, it is very hard to crawl out of it and look ahead to upcoming activities.

In order for a project manager to focus time on proactive activities, he or she will need to reprioritize his or her attention. This probably means not attending some meetings and freeing up time on his or her calendar. There are a few ways to make time for these activities:

- Empower team members to own pieces of work. This will free up time to focus on other activities and will also improve morale and motivation of the team.
- Get help. Some projects create a project management office (PMO) to run the operational aspects of the project, such as financial management, metrics, resource planning, and communications. This allows the project manager to get the information he or she needs to manage the project, but not spend time collecting it.
- Do not go to all meetings. Once the team members are empowered, the project manager should determine the critical meetings he or she needs to attend. This is not to say that he or she shouldn't read meeting minutes or understand the details of the project.
- Block off calendar. Blocking time on the calendar for "office time" or to walk the floors is an effective technique for planning to perform those activities before calendars fill up with meeting invites.

4.1.4 Recognizing That People Will Make the Project Successful

Projects are foundationally made of people doing work. Project managers need to embrace the new model that their role is to facilitate the team working together toward a common goal. This requires an effective relationship with the people on the team and stakeholders supporting the project. There are many examples where people need to be engaged in the project:

- Involving them in the planning of the work
- Empowering them to own pieces of work
- Having them report on time to complete activities
- Supporting them during conflicts or issues
- Uncovering underlying issues during conflicts
- Understanding what motivates them
- Removing obstacles that are preventing them from making progress
- Inspiring and motivating them to perform to their highest potential
- Recognizing them for accomplishments
- Keeping them informed of project information and decisions
- Looking for opportunities to grow their skill sets
- Demonstrating excellence and honesty to the team

Because of the importance of people on the project, the project manager must also invest time in building and fostering relationships with team members and stakeholders.

4.1.5 Be Conscious

A lot of the softer techniques and skills mentioned require that project managers be aware of themselves, their actions, their team, and their environment. This means that project managers must turn off the "autopilot" button in their brain and become much more conscious of themselves and observant of their environment.

Several examples during projects where a project manager needs to be aware of himself or herself include:

- Observing the reactions and involvement of people in meetings in response to the messages that are being said.
- Being aware of his or her presence through how he or she dresses, speaks, and acts.
- Learning by observing others who are effective (or maybe not so effective) in communications, navigating the organization, facilitating meetings, and negotiating difficult situations.
- Asking for feedback on how he or she is performing and working with the team to understand improvement opportunities. The perception from the team is very important to understand because it has a direct influence on the ability to lead them.
- During conflicts, recognizing the different perspectives and motivators for the people involved.

As a result of this self-awareness and recognizing the responses by others, the project manager should then modify his or her approach or interactions accordingly (see next section).

4.1.6 Situational Adaptation

Lastly, the techniques and skills described in this book should not be used in a "one size fits all" model. They need to be applied differently depending on the specific situation and people involved. Table 4.2 gives some examples of how these techniques can be used in different situations during a project.

Beyond the techniques, the leadership skills described in this book also need to be used, depending on the situation and personalities involved. As described in Section 3.5.2, leadership styles should match the commitment

TABLE 4.2

Examples of Techniques during Situations

Area	Project Planning	Project Execution	During Issues
Activity management	• Diligent planning • Involve groups in planning	• Rigor on plan execution • MBWA to get information	• Negotiation • Rapid closure
Relationship focus	• Build relationships	• Foster relationships	• Leverage relationships
Effective communication	• Clarity of plans	• Clarity of progress	• Clarity of issue
Leadership	• Establish trust and credibility	• Motivate and inspire the team	• Champion the team and support them

and competence of the team members. That being said, there are some leadership skills that should never change, including integrity, being genuine, honesty, and championing the team.

There are a few critical skills that can help a project manager to adapt quickly to specific situations:

1. Diligence. Having diligence is important because it provides the ability to be flexible for situations based on preparation. For example, as changes get introduced or there is an unexpected issue on the project, the project manager who has a detailed plan can quickly assess the situation for impact and make a well-informed recommendation or decision. It is very hard to change course and be flexible on a project that does not have tight management over its activities.

2. Judgment. It is the project manager who must determine when to use techniques in specific situations, and having good judgment is critical to do this. Good judgment comes from experience and knowing the different possible outcomes from situations, as well as what has worked and not worked in the past.

3. Experience. Gaining experience in these techniques and skills is really the only way to understand when to best use each one in a way that matches the project manager's style. A project manager needs to recognize that he or she has to constantly build and hone his or her skills, and that he or she is never done learning or gaining practice. Aristotle said it best: "We are what we repeatedly do. Excellence, then, is not an act but a habit."

4.2 SUMMARY OF TECHNIQUES AND SKILLS

Throughout the book there are many techniques and skills suggested that a project manager can use to be effective across various dimensions of project delivery. This section summarizes them in sets of checklists that a project manager can use for different situations on his or her projects. The checklists also align the techniques and skills with the four main categories of skills that described in Chapter 3:

1. Additional rigor
2. Consultative approach
3. Management of information
4. Leading the team

Table 4.3 summarizes the set of foundational skills that a project manager should practice and continue to develop. These are skills that are not specific to a situation, but rather core skills that project managers should possess.

TABLE 4.3

Foundational Skills

Technique/Skill	Rigor	Consult	Info	Lead
Be organized, which will help manage the work and provide clarity to stakeholders	X			
Understand standard deliverables used in project execution	X			
Continue to build competencies around technical and business acumen	X			
Persuasion (ethos, pathos, and logos)		X		
Presence and confidence		X		
Successful facilitation of meetings		X		
Effective negotiation		X		
Listening and being seen as approachable		X		
Self-management		X		
Understand the organization and build coalitions		X		
Present information well		X	X	
Focus on key messages in communications			X	
Motivate the team and recognize excellence				X
Set the example and recognize that team members are always watching				X
Look for opportunities to empower team members				X

TABLE 4.4

Project Planning Techniques

Technique/Skill	Rigor	Consult	Info	Lead
Understand and plan for activities, including additional stakeholders and groups	X			
Plan for small units of work and consider using earned value to monitor progress	X			
Plan for rework	X			
Define and document the project management approach	X			
Consider creating a project management office	X			
Use historical information to incorporate and plan for lessons learned	X			
Ensure that all plans align (resources, cost, schedule, and plan)	X			
Document the critical path activities on the project plan	X			
Use methodology deliverables and standard checklists	X			
Plan for deliverable reviews	X			
Identify and obtain resources with the right skill sets	X			
Provide clarity of project roles and accountabilities	X			
Determine backup strategy for key resources	X			
Consider using schedule contingency	X			
Define the proper project metrics	X			
Engage resource areas early	X	X		
Involve resources and experts in planning; look for opportunities to empower team members	X	X		
Start building relationships with team members and stakeholders; understand their motivators		X		X
Have an effective communication plan with all stakeholders identified			X	

Table 4.4 lists the techniques to be used up front on a project as it is being planned. Most of the items on the checklist require appropriate rigor, but there are some "softer" activities to be considered as well.

Table 4.5 identifies techniques to be used during the execution portion of the project. This is usually the longest part of the project, so it is important to keep revisiting these techniques so that they don't lose momentum and impact as the project continues in a day-to-day mode.

Table 4.6 captures some of the key techniques to be used when there are items that require escalation and management attention. The keys are to identify the challenges early and present fact-based information to management.

Table 4.7 lists the techniques that can be used to prepare for and conduct meetings. These are a combination of diligence around planning for the

TABLE 4.5

Project Executing Techniques

Technique/Skill	Rigor	Consult	Info	Lead
Focus on value-added deliverables	X			
Conduct deliverable reviews	X			
Leverage experts as much as possible	X			
Rigor around the plan and upcoming activities, including tracking of estimate to complete	X			
Maintain constant diligence on operational items	X			
Assign responsibilities and hold people accountable for deliverables and results	X			
Look to make or facilitate timely decisions	X			
Use metrics to understand project health	X			
Present facts and recomendations for management decisions	X			
Foster relationships with team members and stakeholders		X		
Get visibility of project health			X	
Communicate often with stakeholders			X	
Continue to recognize, motivate, and inspire the team				X
Champion the team				X

TABLE 4.6

Managing Items That Require Attention

Technique/Skill	Rigor	Consult	Info	Lead
Leverage relationships and MBWA to understand challenges early		X	X	
Use metrics and collect appropriate information	X		X	
Presell ideas		X		
Present facts	X	X		
Support the team's recommendations				X

TABLE 4.7

Preparing for and Conducting Meetings

Technique/Skill	Rigor	Consult	Info	Lead
Have a clear agenda and distribute materials beforehand	X		X	
Understand audience and stakeholders	X		X	
Focus on the messages for the meeting			X	
Facilitate meeting and present suggestions effectively		X	X	
Be conscious of reactions in the room and how information is received		X		
Document outcomes of the meeting	X			

TABLE 4.8

Activities to Perform during the Day

Technique/Skill	Rigor	Consult	Info	Lead
Look ahead at the plan to understand upcoming tasks, key dates, and resource needs	X			
Look at upcoming meetings to ensure adequate preparation	X			
Follow up on any open item	X			
Review metrics to understand progress and risk areas	X			
Practice MBWA to understand status and gather risks		X	X	
Send any updates needed to stakeholders			X	
Recognize excellence				X
Inspire through actions				X

TABLE 4.9

Managing Conflicts

Technique/Skill	Rigor	Consult	Info	Lead
Use facts and data and do not make it personal	X			
Practice self-management and don't overreact to the situation; seek to understand all information		X		
Facilitate successful outcomes		X		
Demonstrate support for the team members				X

meeting and effective communication skills during the meeting to achieve the desired results.

Table 4.8 lists techniques that should be considered daily activities for a project manager. Time should be allocated on a regular basis to perform these activities. Blocking off time first thing in the morning is a good way to make this a habit.

Table 4.9 lists several techniques that can be used during conflicts that arise on the project.

References

Blanchard, Kenneth, Hershey, Paul, and Johnson, Dewey. 1997. *Management of organizational behavior*. 9th ed. New York: Prentice Hall.

Bradberry, Travis, and Greaves, Jean. 2005. *The emotional intelligence quick book*. New York: Simon and Schuster.

Computer Economics Inc. 2009. *IT spending and staffing benchmarks*.

Covey, Stephen. 1989. *The seven habits of highly effective people*. New York: Simon & Schuster.

Erl, Thomas. 2005. *Service-oriented architecture: Concepts, technology, and design*. Upper Saddle River, NJ: Prentice Hall.

French, John and Raven, Bertram. 1959. The bases of social power. In *Studies in social power*, ed. D. Cartwright. Ann Arbor: University of Michigan Press, pages 150–167.

Goleman, Daniel. 1998. *Working with emotional intelligence*. New York: Bantam Books.

Lewis, James P. 1998. *Team-based project management*. New York: AMACOM.

Newell, Michael, and Grashina, Marina. 2003. *The project management question and answer book*. New York: AMACON.

Index